Praise for *Rapid Growth*

'Val Wright makes the complex simple. She zones in on what is happening and lightbulbs go off that truly allow you to grow your business in the right way.' JENNIFER ANAYA, SVP MARKETING, INGRAM MICRO INC.

'I have read many business and leadership books and never has one been so unique, practical and immediately applicable as *Rapid Growth, Done Right*. Every executive should read it.' ANDREW CLARKE, CEO, FRANCESCA'S

'This is the ultimate guide for how technical, creative and business teams can work together so that they are all talking the same language. Val Wright's advice and toolkit will help leaders of all disciplines improve their ability to lead innovative and fast-growing companies.' LANCE RALLS, CIO, BELKIN INTERNATIONAL

'As a creative business executive in the entertainment industry I love experimenting with new ideas. This advice provides rapid practical examples that I can immediately apply.' MIKE TUNNICLIFFE, FORMER EVP, HEAD OF UNIVERSAL MUSIC GROUP AND BRANDS USA

'This advice is so concise and powerful. Just what executives need to hear right now to grow their business during times of change.' CAROLINA STAVROSITU, FORMER EXECUTIVE DIRECTOR, CONTENT MARKETING, TIME

Rapid Growth, Done Right

Lead, influence and innovate for success

Val Wright

KoganPage

First published in Great Britain and the United States in 2020 by Kogan Page Limited

2nd Floor, 45 Gee Street	122 W 27th St, 10th Floor	4737/23 Ansari Road
London	New York, NY 10001	Daryaganj
EC1V 3RS	USA	New Delhi 110002
United Kingdom		India

www.koganpage.com

Kogan Page books are printed on paper from sustainable forests.

ISBNs

Hardback	978 1 78966 408 9
Paperback	978 1 78966 405 8
Ebook	978 1 78966 406 5

British Library Cataloguing-in-Publication Data

A CIP record for this book is available from the British Library.

Library of Congress Cataloging-in-Publication Number

2020007985

Typeset by Integra Software Services, Pondicherry
Print production managed by Jellyfish
Printed and bound by CPI Group (UK) Ltd, Croydon CR0 4YY

To Peter Shankman,
Thank you for your podcast and book, Faster Than Normal,
which helped me discover the gift of my neurodiverse brain and
ADHD diagnosis while writing this book.

To Dr Susan Reedy,
Your brilliant insights as my therapist and confidant has
strengthened my mental health to new heights.

Contents

Preface

Companies that catapult growth have one common trait: they pay attention to the symbiotic relationship between their technical, creative and business minds. Too often these three are unintentionally disconnected. Overhearing conversations between marketing, business and technical people can often make you feel as though you have landed in a foreign country and are listening to someone speaking a different language, and when you can't be understood you try to speak more slowly and loudly, but to no avail. This confusion does not have to continue. A deliberate focus on how you lead, make decisions and inspire inside and outside your company will provide the translation required to accelerate growth and innovation.

A business rapidly grows when leaders connect creative, technical and business minds. Creative minds design and envision the growth engine, the technical team builds the engine and makes it work, and the business side of the company makes sure that the engine will make money and beat the competition. The most successful companies make this happen in a symbiotic, iterative and parallel way. Leaders orchestrate everyone, building on each other's ideas, challenging each other, helping each other dream big but stay grounded, and rapidly take ideas into action. Then the magical symbiosis happens, and endless growth is effortless.

The expertise of your CEO is the pivotal power of your organization, and the rest of your leadership team need complementary talents that circle the CEO at the right cadence and force. Companies that are too focused and heavy on technical expertise will lose creativity. Companies that are too creative may not have a profitable solution. Companies that weight decisions purely on business metrics won't delight customers and create exponential growth through innovation. The Innovation Trifecta provides the symbiosis so that you can create innovative products and services that your customers will love.

Rapid growth in companies happens when the leadership team, creative, technical and business minds are in their perfect job and have a symbiotic bond. Not every story in this book is perfect. You will also hear unplugged stories and lessons learned from successful executives who experienced the ultimate corporate sacrifice: getting fired or pushed out.

Using examples and interviews from executives across companies large and small, from Mars, Xbox, Starbucks, Amazon and the LA Rams to start-ups and mid-size companies, this book will help you learn:

- how to evaluate and increase your power of influence;
- why it is essential to rapidly put the right people in the right roles;
- to translate and communicate across creative, technical and business teams;
- the steps to build an innovative strategy and company;
- new approaches for increasing your creative appreciation;
- different methods for enhancing your technical prowess;
- alternative ways to improve your business understanding;
- how to increase the quantity and quality of ideas to accelerate innovation;
- to unlock the barriers to fast decision-making;
- how you can successfully work with a genius;
- new ways to implement fast results.

Follow the guidance in this book and you will no longer hear complaints like, 'If only the technical team would understand how we need to build a business model that will disrupt our industry'; 'If only the creative team would realize their ideas are technically impossible'; 'If only the business team would realize there will be no sustainable profit unless we have a creative experience that our customers love'. Instead, you will have learned new methods and have adopted new words that just work in common scenarios for rapid business growth.

Now let's explore how to do that the right way.

Acknowledgements

This book is a culmination of the real time laboratory that is my work as I speak at conferences, advise executive teams, create innovation laboratories and run workshops around the world.

Taking the idea from a collection of thoughts and ideas into my second book would never have happened without the following people:

My inner circle of executive advisors who reciprocate with feedback for me just when I need it: Andrea Leigh, Andrew Clarke, Dina Marovich, Jennifer Anaya, Julie Bernard, Kate Scolnick, Lori Wright, Lance Ralls, Mike Tunnicliffe, Ronalee Zarate-Bayani, Tara Moeller and Tracy Reilly.

Alan Weiss, my strategic advisor, author of over 60 books and godfather of the most esteemed community of consultants, speakers, and authors in the world. Thank you, Alan, for continuing to draw back the curtains so I can better see the true possibilities of what I can achieve, your wise counsel and wit is priceless.

Chris Cudmore, Martin Hill, Susi Lowndes, Ruth Reisenberger, Jaini Haria, Courtney Dramis, Vanessa Rueda and the team at Kogan Page. Your detailed feedback and insights resulted in a book that will accelerate innovation and growth for companies around the world.

My husband Andy and daughters Naomi, Keira and Olivia whose endless faith, infinite energy and strong support for me gives me renewed enthusiasm every day.

About the author

Val Wright is a recognized global innovation and leadership expert. The clients who have requested her help include Starbucks, LinkedIn, Amazon, Microsoft, Gartner, *Financial Times*, Belkin International, Ingram Micro and the Los Angeles Lakers. Val's corporate experience includes tenures during dramatic growth periods at Amazon, Land Rover, House of Fraser and Xbox. She is an inductee into the Million Dollar Consultant® Hall of Fame. Her publications include Amazon bestselling book *Thoughtfully Ruthless: The Key to Exponential Growth* and regular contributions with CNBC, BBC, Fox Business News, Sirius XM, iHeartRadio, Inc. Magazine, Bloomberg, *Los Angeles Times* and Today.

CHAPTER ONE

Evaluating your personal power to innovate

Innovation is not random, lucky or haphazard, yet many companies leave it to chance. Understanding how innovation can grind to a halt and knock confident leaders sideways allows us to prevent it from happening to us. In this chapter we will explore what happens when technical, business or creative power takes over and conscious or unconscious decisions about the speed and impact of innovation occurs. You have to start with you. You can immediately predict how likely you are to succeed by understanding how strong your power of influence is. You will learn how to understand how strong and deep your influence is as you hear stories from executives at Amazon, Snapchat, HBO and Microsoft about how they have improved their impact. You will leave with a clear assessment of the strength of your influence and pragmatic steps you can immediately implement to increase your innovation impact.

Why creativity is crucial

How did Amazon go from selling books and cheap socks to selling designer fashion, cloud services and healthcare? The differentiator that turned Amazon into the multidimensional collection of businesses it is today is how its leaders led, influenced and innovated. After founding Amazon, Jeff Bezos continued his relentless disruption into the world of fashion by acquiring high-end-designer online store Shopbop in 2006 and Zappos in 2009. He wanted to take over the business of fashion in a wide-reaching way, but there was one crucial component missing: Amazon had never had to market before. They didn't have a typical marketing department, nor did they invest in advertising. Customers would land on their site and search for the precise book that they wanted, which is nothing like consumers looking for clothing, shoes or other accessories. The fashion business is driven by the creative lure of the gorgeous advert, pretty picture, or beautiful photograph. Amazon never had to worry before about how to take a picture of a book with the perfect lighting – but the precision that goes into shoe photography is something else!

Jeff Wilke, currently CEO of Worldwide Consumer at Amazon, but at the time SVP Consumer Business at Amazon, knew he had a crucial talent gap. If he had not been aware of this, it could have brought Amazon's dreams of retail disruption to a swift end, but instead it became the pivotal moment that won the fashion race. He chose to hire an industry veteran who had successful tenures at Gap and Old Navy. The first online shoe store Piperlime was the brainchild of Cathy Beaudoin, and she was to join the fastest-growing retailer of all time and disrupt the most archaic industry of all.

Amazon's fashion business didn't just create a multibillion-dollar business for Amazon, it also became the growth accelerator for many executives who went on to become CEOs, executives and board members of companies, including Zulily CEO Jeff Yurcisin, Bergoff Goodman President Darcy Penick, Digital VP of L'Oreal Maria Plitas, PepsiCo SVP of Innovation Daren Hull, and Barry's Bootcamp CMO Melissa Weiss.

How you can rapidly lose first place

Nobody could have guessed that Blackberry would go from 50 per cent market share to less than 1 per cent in under three years. It could have been a very different story for Blackberry. How does a market leader fall from grace so badly that they have to admit defeat and announce a last-ditch effort to sell their company? According to a report by Gartner, Inc., Blackberry's market share plummeted from 50 per cent in 2009 to less than 3 per cent five years later. How did Blackberry lose the hearts and wallets of their customers? During this decline,

Nobody could have guessed that Blackberry would go from 50 per cent market share to less than 1 per cent in under three years.

why didn't any of the rumored acquisitions of Blackberry by Microsoft, HTC, Amazon or Samsung materialize?

What makes one company more innovative than another? It is more than just size, leadership or technology; the culture that you create and reinforce every day will drive rapid and long-lasting. The culture at Blackberry was tumultuous. Thorsten Heins knew Blackberry inside out when he took the CEO role in January 2012, yet he still claimed that the company did not need to change and there was nothing wrong when he was appointed. He was formerly chief operating officer at RIM, Blackberry's parent company. If you appoint an internal CEO, you need to surround them with disruptive thinkers and diverse views to balance their thinking. Had Blackberry done this, their dilemma may well have been solved. Chapter 5 will explore just how to prevent group-think and team mini-me.

In business today, there is an aspirational trend and an unhealthy obsession with failing fast, failing often and rewarding failure. Failure should not be a badge of honor, but successful companies know how to name it, deconstruct it, learn and move on. Blackberry took too long to acknowledge that two significant products, Playbook and Q10, were not successful. Chapter 3 provides a toolkit for deconstructing and learning from successes and failures that every company can immediately apply.

Innovative companies make sure that their employees' energy and time is focused on customers, products and profits. You only have to listen in to informal conversations in hallways and corridors of companies around the world to find out what people are talking about. Too much energy wasted on rumor, speculation and hearsay is a major distraction. Blackberry has been criticized for how they executed layoffs, handled executive behavior issues and failed to target those underperforming or coasting along in their roles.[1] Communicating across technical, creative and business teams requires thought and focus. Chapter 5 is packed with examples and proven techniques for unlocking capacity, showing you how to speak and write to your employees, shareholders, investors and customers.

How to understand your power of influence

Picture your three most powerful supporters at work. This could be your boss, your board chair, your CFO or one of your peers. Now imagine all three of them quitting the organization at precisely the same time in the same week. All of a sudden, your product launch, new strategy or acquisition plans are in serious jeopardy – not because your ideas are poor, or your technology is inferior, or because your customers won't buy your next big product idea, but because your supporters have left the building.

There are innovation labs all around the world forming brilliant revolutionary ways to blow the minds of customers, radically improve profits and disrupt market share. But if those ideas don't have executive support, then you might as well not bother innovating in the first place.

Here are two company examples where innovation didn't get to market because of lack of executive support.

Microsoft Courier: a dual-screen tablet

I worked in Microsoft's Entertainment and Devices division in 2010 when the dual-screen touch screen tablet (code-named Courier) was created. This was before the first Apple iPad was launched, and the CEO at the time, Steve Ballmer, chose not to take the innovation incubation to full production. An investigation by CNET later revealed that Ballmer was too concerned with how it would impact the existing operating system, Windows. With chairman and founder Bill Gates's support, the prototype was cancelled. Nine years later, in 2019, Microsoft launched its Surface NEO, a similar dual-screen tablet that echoes the design of the original Courier.

Marconi's Future Refrigerator that will order your groceries

In 1999 British telecommunication giant Marconi had a prototype for a refrigerator that could automatically order your milk and cheese for you. During my tenure in their global managed services division, I watched tireless pitch after pitch to take the concept out to customers. The innovation team at the time could not get the funding to make their futuristic vision reality. Now, nearly two decades later, the technology is starting to enter advanced kitchens around the world. In 2019, Brandessence Market Research estimated that the smart refrigeration market will reach $1 billion by 2025.[2] The technology was available for Marconi to develop it in 1999, but lack of top executive belief prevented it from becoming a reality. Marconi suffered a catastrophic downfall and its share price crashed in one year from £12.50 to 29 pence.[3] Perhaps if innovations like the smart refrigerator had been funded, it could have turned the tide and divested opportunities to new markets.

The Dyson difference

In sharp contrast, James Dyson spent 15 years trying to launch his revolutionary vacuum cleaners. In an essay he wrote for Canada's *Globe and Mail* he proudly shares how it took 5,127 attempts before his company got it right.[4] The crucial difference here was that Dyson was a privately held company where Sir James Dyson owned 100 per cent of the business, so patience and time were two components he had in abundance. But for the majority of leaders, executives and team members, the crucial thread in unlocking innovation and rapid growth lies with you as a leader. Rapid growth occurs when you can rapidly incubate, launch and grow new products. If they are left on the drawing board or in the innovation lab, your efforts are futile. It's your job to ensure that your latest initiative gains executive support. The key is to understand how strong your power of executive influence is. It is vital to nurture and maintain those relationships, even though it is easy to forget to prioritize them.

It only takes two of your strongest executive champions to say 'I quit!' in quick succession for you to find yourself without your steadfast supporters. Before you know it, you are drifting out to sea, alone in your boat, without the necessary executive lifeguards keeping an eye out for your successful voyage and safe return. This is why you will see a rush of leadership changes when a top executive leaves an organization.

Two of my Fortune 500 executive clients recently got promoted, both had their responsibilities either double or triple in size, and both had one of those giant executive leaps that included a prestigious letter change in their titles. We had previously focused on their circle of influence and the need to rapidly gain supporters and allies; for each of them their work has paid off with improved results for their companies along with personal recognition. Their division's rapid growth was not impacted by leadership changes at the executive team level. Could you say the same if your supporters were to leave tomorrow? How intentional are you in gaining and maintaining executive support? How can you increase *your* influence?

Your influence bullseye: how to build your impact

Here is a fast way of developing an influence strategy that will increase the probability of your getting promoted, having your projects run smoothly, continuing the rapid growth of your business and receiving an abundance of support all around you.

Using the simple model of a bullseye target (see Figure 1.1), think of the three to five people in your company who have your success at their fingertips. Who are those people? They are your power influencers. They're the people who can make or break your career; they make the difference between your bonus being incredible, just okay or downright terrible.

Power influencers are at the center, but you must not make the mistake that many make: trying to go after those people directly. You could try and connect and spend time with them, but the reality is that they have too many competing priorities for their time and energy. Their seniority and influence mean

FIGURE 1.1 Circle of influence bullseye

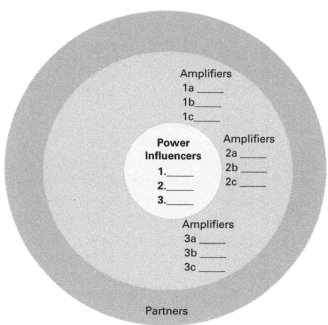

that you are one of many who has them in the bullseye. Even though they hold your success in their hands, do not chase them. Instead, chase their trusted advisors.

Who influences your power influencers? Those are the people with whom they have really strong relationships. Those are the people whom I call *amplifiers*. Focus on the amplifiers, because they have more access and are more likely to spend time and energy on you. They will influence your power influencers. Amplifiers provide a strong return on your efforts with them. Given they are influencing very senior executives, they are likely to be well connected and can help you in multiple ways.

Finally, on the outside of these three concentric rings, your *partners* are the people whom you work with on a daily basis. If I ask any leader to open up their calendar, many have a large portion of their time packed with the partners that they deal with day-to-day. Look at your calendar; it will reveal a lot.

A retail industry executive, with whom I was working, called me and said, 'It happened, Val. They've all quit on me.' Five of his most important power influencers departed within a two-week window. Six months before this, with a pending acquisition looming, we had predicted that this was going to happen, and he had put a number of things in place, including building relationships, to make sure that his current power influencers and his new power influencers were replaced. If that wasn't enough change, a week later his boss quit, and then a week later there was a new CEO. With these multiple levels of change happening, he was given an interim boss. But because he had not done a good job of managing the relationship with this specific person, that was a little rocky.

The most successful leaders dedicate time and attention to their influence plan. When you do this, it helps to ensure that, regardless of the change or turmoil happening in the executive ranks, you are able to continue to build those relationships, allowing you to be successful regardless of who is above or alongside you. In my day-to-day coaching and client work I hear standard comments about people's quickly-changing circumstances. Situations like the following should inspire you to focus on your influence plan:

The most successful leaders dedicate time and attention to their influence plan.

- 'I've had four bosses in the last four years.'
- 'The person who hired me is now gone, and I kind of feel like I'm out to sea in a sailboat with no life jacket. I'm a bit worried what's going to happen when the waves start getting choppy.'
- 'My new boss is going to bring in her colleagues from her previous company.'
- 'We just got acquired, the founders will be leaving soon, and now I have to start again building relationships.'
- 'I've been too busy building and launching products, and I haven't prioritized building relationships.'

Which of the above have happened to you or are likely to happen soon?

THE EXPONENTIAL IMPACT OF YOUR AMPLIFIERS

Let's consider one power influencer that you've chosen. Now think about their amplifiers, and then ask yourself whether each of those amplifiers is supportive of you. Are they a strong advocate who really gets you, your strategy and what you're trying to do? Or is the relationship a bit iffy and you're not quite sure? Are they at odds with you? Do they completely disagree with you? Did you have that one conflict over that one business strategy and now there's not a good relationship there? Of course, it's also possible that you don't have much of a relationship with them, so you don't even know if they are positive, negative or neutral about you.

With these points in mind, you can take your amplifiers and assess them, and then put together a specific plan for each amplifier. One executive that I was working with had a peer who held a significant amount of influence for the technical projects that he was trying to launch. We spent a lot of time unpacking what it was that was causing this relationship to be tense. The proven method for influencing people to be receptive to your point of view is to appeal to what they care about. What is in it for them? If you don't know that, you need to find out. Chapter 5 helps you understand how to build this influence across your creative, technical and business peers, and gives you specific tools to accelerate the development and launch of your new products and initiatives.

The most powerful question you can ask to help build connections is to ask for advice. Robert Cialdini, the master of influence, taught me this when I worked with him at Alan Weiss's Thought Leadership Summit. He shared that the most powerful way to get help from others is to ask for advice, not a favor. For some leaders that may feel a bit uncomfortable, because it requires vulnerability and a willingness to ask for, listen to, and take advice – which not all executives like to do. But asking for advice builds influence and connection, and in turn that really helps you build relationships.

YOUR DAILY PARTNERS

The third circle in the 'influence bullseye' is partners. One question that I hear a lot is how to approach the partners that people work with day-to-day. My candid response is not to worry about them. Focus on the amplifiers first, and then your power influencers. This is because there is so much more return on investment effort with those relationships. If all of your power influencers are great supporters and your amplifiers are all on your page, then it's time to focus on your partners. But I've never seen an executive in that position, because things change so rapidly. Unless one of your partners is a noisy outlier, don't prioritize them.

Your influence action plan

1 Identify who has the greatest impact on your own success and your team's:
   - **Power Influencers (PI's):** These are the top two or three senior executives who most impact your success and reputation.
   - **Amplifiers:** These are the people who have the ear of the PI's and can have a positive, neutral or negative impact on how the PI's perceive you.
   - **Partners:** These are the people you work with day-to-day; they are important, but it is easy to get distracted and absorbed with them.
2 Pick the power influencer that you need to change most rapidly your relationship with and determine how you can improve that relationship.
3 Focus on their amplifiers and identify ways in which you can use their influence to increase the support you get directly from the power influencer.

4 For each PI and amplifier, answer the following:

- **Background** – How you know them, past results/ relationship.
- **Status** – Supporter, contrarian, in-sync, unknown.
- **Key insights** – What do you know about your current relationship that you need to consider?
- **Their style** – What gets their attention, drives them crazy, sparks their interest, triggers their passion or frustrations?
- **Your interactions** – What formal and informal interactions do you have with them now and what do you expect in the future?
- **Barriers** – What perceived or real barriers exist that need to be overcome?
- **Strategy** – What is your three-step influence plan? (Feel free to pick just one or two steps if that will be sufficient. But choose no more than three.)

An influence plan that catapulted European expansion

A chief technology officer client had been working on these influence strategies as part of the foundation of his start-up's growth. His team was able to rapidly deploy technology that improved the revenue and profitability of their customers, but they needed investment to scale and grow faster. He knew that in order to be successful he needed the support of the executive team and the board as they raised another round of funding from investors. By developing strong relationships with the external investment community and building confidence with the board by influencing their amplifiers, he not only expanded the technology initiatives but was also approached to be the president of the company. This allowed him to rapidly make investment decisions to expand into Europe because he had built the confidence of the board and investors when he was deep in his technology leadership role.

Why your personal valuation impacts your company valuation

A divisional president that I was working with called me, exasperated. He said, 'Val, I cannot believe he got that job. He should never have gotten that job. I worked with him three years ago, and he should never have gotten that job.' As we unpacked it, we realized that while the promoted executive's achievements weren't that great, he did excel at showcasing his achievements. Talking with my client, we discovered that his own specific focus had been solely concentrated internally to the detriment of his external reputation. An outcome from this coaching was how to do a better job of showcasing his achievements internally but also externally. How well you promote your achievements externally can affect your company valuation, who wants to invest in you, which strategic partners will want to do business with you and how rapidly you can grow.

How high is your personal valuation today?

The output of your power of influence impacts how you are valued. Your valuation is like the stock valuation or share price of a company and this will go up and down throughout your career. In fact, you have two valuations, an internal valuation and an external valuation (see Figure 1.2). Consider your internal valuation right now. Is it high? Is it right? Could it be a lot better? Now think about your external valuation. Is your reputation outside the company stronger than it is inside the company?

Your valuation is like the stock valuation or share price of a company and this will go up and down throughout your career.

Depending on where you are in your career and depending on where you have focused your time and energy, those two numbers may be quite different.

This internal valuation will help you evaluate just where you need to focus your influence to support the rapid growth of your

FIGURE 1.2 Your personal stock valuation

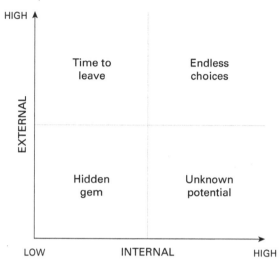

company. Done right, you will grow your business; done wrong, you will waste time in the wrong area and you will not build the partnerships, receive the right investments or attract other brilliant minds to work with you.

While this book is more of a growth catapult for your business, if you don't rapidly put the right people in the right roles, you will not be growing your business in the right way. It reminds me of my first job as a management trainee at House of Fraser in their Birmingham store. Our mantra there was putting the right products in the right place at the right time and at the right price. On the retail floor, on my first assignment selling televisions and music systems, I fast discovered that the store made most of its profit in six short weeks of the year. I saw how precarious profits were and just how many temporary employees we hired for short-term work to meet the holiday-shoppers' demands. I distinctly remember the frustration of the menswear department manager, who hadn't hired the right salespeople for the recently launched Ralph Lauren department. Sales were impacted that he could never recover, his annual profit goal was missed, and he lost out on a valuable commission. Other department managers in the store could hire faster and did; they had a magnetism that drew in the very salespeople they needed to hire.

Just how magnetic are you and will it accelerate or slow down your rapid growth? (See Figure 1.3.)

The magnetically brilliant executive

'I am too old to get on a board. I have left it until it's too late, Val!' You might think that a 95-year-old said this, but it was a remarkably successful technology executive, about half that age. I explained that nothing could be further from the truth and that I knew many boards would be delighted to have her expertise. The issue was not one of age, but of how magnetic her brilliance was.

I hear a comparison complaint frequently, and it alarms me. I'm told that executives with less experience and limited results achieve greater success. You can measure just how magnetic

FIGURE 1.3 The magnetic executive

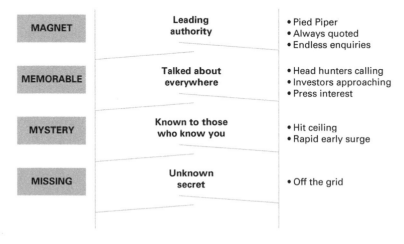

your brilliance is with the magnetic executive assessment. How magnetic are you?

Four stages of the magnetic executive

• Stage 1: Missing

You are a best-kept secret. People don't know you exist. You are off the grid, and nobody knows what you've accomplished and where you accomplished it. You have complete radio silence about your work life.

• Stage 2: Mystery

If you are a mystery, you are known to those who know you. People within your first set of connections know you very well, but you quickly hit a ceiling at this level. Think back to five or ten years ago in your career when you probably knew a lot of people in your network who could hire you. Naturally, as you rise up the career ladder, taking on increased roles and scope (including perhaps a growing company and increased size and scale of investors), you need an upgraded network if you want relationships with people who can hire you, place you on a board or invest in your company. Without that upgraded network, you are going to hit a ceiling. Many leaders hit this ceiling at Director and VP level inside large companies. Executives also find it easy to get their first CIO, CMO or other role reporting to the CEO, but the second one doesn't come as easily unless you have upgraded your network ahead of time.

• Stage 3: Memorable

When you do break through the ceiling, you become memorable. At this stage you are talked about everywhere, and you have headhunters calling you. You are well known. Random people call you, but you don't know exactly where they found you. The calls might be for press, for quotes, for speaking or for board advisory. It could also be someone asking, 'Can I pick your brain? I want to follow your path and do what you did.' When that starts happening, you'll know you're memorable.

- Stage 4: Magnetic

When you're a magnet, you are a leading authority. You are at the top of your game. I call these leaders the Pied Pipers, because everyone follows them. They move companies and they can immediately fill their leadership team with all the people that they have from all those other places because they've been so good at maintaining each one. If you're magnetic, you are always quoted and receive endless enquiries. It is easy to find out your point of view on relevant topics because you are interviewed and featured everywhere.

Real-life magnetic leaders

You've probably thought of a few well-known magnetic leaders: people like Richard Branson, Jeff Bezos, Bill Gates and Sheryl Sandberg. They are magnetic leaders, but they now have endless teams, resources and money to make their magnetism happen. I am going to profile real executives and leaders who exemplify what it means to be a brilliantly magnetic leader, leading to rapid growth and unprecedented business results.

Here are three real-life reachable examples of those at the top of their game who will share their stories and experience throughout this book:

1 **Shane Small, executive creative director at Facebook and Snapchat, founder of highest-backed Kickstarter, Exploding Kittens.** Shane created the $8.7 million-backed Kickstarter campaign with Exploding Kittens. He is the creative genius behind new TV shows for Sony and Hulu, and he invented interactive wearable clothing decades before it was a trend. He's worked on gaming devices, a mobile charades game and many more that are likely still a top secret. Just sitting next to Shane for five minutes will make you feel more creative. His energy and inspiration are contagious.

2 **Otto Berkes, co-founder of Xbox, former CTO at HBO, CTO and Innovation Lab creator at CA Technologies.** If you watch HBO GO or play Xbox, you have Otto to thank for that. Otto transformed HBO from the inside out as he designed and launched HBO GO, and he created a VC company within CA Technologies that had a success rate twice the industry average. He has even written a book about his experience, *Digitally Remastered.*

3 **Ronalee Zarate-Bayani, CMO of LA Rams, formerly at Hershey's, Visa and Taco Bell.** Ronalee is right at the heart of the biggest development that the West coast will see this decade. The home of the new LA Rams stadium is part of a 300-acre city being built. Imagine that as the driving force for your company strategy! Ronalee has strategically moved between consumer goods, financial services and fast-food industries before landing with the LA Rams. A simply brilliant speaker, with a unique blend of business and creative thinking, she has a trail of marketing experts who follow her as though she's the Pied Piper of marketing.

How to know when your network is dehydrated

There is a simple way to immediately know if your network has expired. Executives can be overtaken by their peers and not realize it until it is almost too late. Rapid Growth Done Wrong happens when you are focusing on delivering brilliant products and services for your company and you forget to prioritize yourself. You can likely still catch it and turn it around, but first you have to assess whether you need a drop or two of water or a whole bucket to quench the thirst of your dehydrated network. Pay attention to which of the following apply to you:

1 **You no longer know people who can hire you.** Five years ago, those in your network could hire you. As your trajectory

increases, you have to upgrade your circle of who knows you at the right altitude. That population changes the more successful you are.

2 **You are giving more than you are receiving.** Of course, you want to support others earlier in their career journey, but is it weighted the wrong way? If you aren't getting as much as you are sharing, then it's time to make some changes.

3 **You realize 'precision divorcing' is a necessity.** Who in your network do you need to spend less time and energy with to enable you to free up more time to focus on those you need to support your company's growth?

4 **Your peers are landing bigger jobs**, board seats, speaking engagements, media interviews, and winning recognition awards.

Andrew Clarke, CEO of francesca's women's retail stores, quickly realized he was at the mystery phase when he started looking for his next role. Here is what he shared with me:

I am definitely a mystery to my network, and my external Personal Share Value was lower than I realized. From my move from President of Kmart, which was my first General Management role, I became focused on turning that business around, which I did, but it was to the detriment of my positioning myself with my new peers. When I first moved to the US, I also entered a networking black hole, I became out of sync, whereas my connections and peer group in Europe in the fashion industry at New Look and from Marks & Spencer were strong. I just didn't prioritize my time when I landed in the US. I noticed that my peers were getting appointed to roles that I would have been perfect for, but as I was unknown, executive roles were getting created and executive candidates were put forward. I was not considered for them because I was a mystery to those who could hire me. Now I am in catch-up mode to close that deficit, which can't simply be done overnight or in a few weeks. I definitely didn't realize the value of having a network and making sure it was one that I consulted and invested in regularly until I was looking for my next opportunity. Everybody knows the companies I've worked for. They're public companies, so people know the results I've delivered, but they don't attribute them to me and my brand, because they don't really know anything about me. My advice is to make sure you invest in keeping your network at the right level before you actually need it, otherwise you have to invest in playing catch-up for the time that you lost.

Candid feedback for any executive

In case you are still not certain whether you need to rehydrate your network, consider the following:

- Your future employees don't want to work for a mystery person.
- Your investors pay attention to your reputation and industry impact.
- Your digital reputation is just as important as your reputation in the real world.
- Your company and personal rapid growth may be impacted if you don't share your recent brilliant company results online.
- When you move regions or countries, building your influence locally is critical.

It is lonely at the top, but it doesn't have to be

You'll Never Walk Alone is the motto of English soccer team Liverpool Football Club. Their new CEO Peter Moore was able to use his power of influence to define and find his perfect executive role as he returned to his hometown of Liverpool after 35 years in the United States, following successful executive roles at Sega, Reebok, Xbox and Electronic Arts. It is a fitting reminder that regardless of your role, whether a board member, executive, first-time manager or fresh out of school, your career and business life can be lonely.

There is a reason the phrase 'it is lonely at the top' is overused – because it is true. The more senior you get, the lonelier it can become. But it doesn't have to be that way. How you influence, lead and innovate is a journey you do not have to take alone. This book will provide you with the mindset, toolkit and real-life stories to allow you to rapidly grow your business and career in the right way. You are already 33 per cent of the way there, because the first of three critical parts of rapidly learning how to grow is by asking, accepting and applying advice. It's what I call the 'Triple A' approach to rapid learning, and you have completed step one: **ASK**-ing for advice by reading this book. Here are the three steps:

> There is a reason the phrase 'it is lonely at the top' is overused – because it is true.

- **Ask:** Get expert help from those who have been there, done that and achieved results.
- **Accept:** Without overthinking, consider and then accept an alternative approach.
- **Apply:** Move rapidly to test, trial, experiment, and just DO more than THINK. If you write it down, you improve the probability that you will take action. If you share that action with someone else, your success rate increases further. And if you DON'T take action in the next 12 hours after reading this chapter, your probability of ever taking action diminishes substantially. Take advantage of the Rapid Recap at the end of this and every chapter by using it to create a checklist and action plan for yourself. You can find a complete set of rapid recaps and additional bonus tools to download and use at www.rapidgrowthdoneright.com.

Next, in Chapter 2, we will explore why it is essential to have the right people in the right job so that you can build rapid growth. It starts with looking in the mirror and asking if you are the right person to be growing your business rapidly, and what to do about it if you are not.

CHAPTER 1 RAPID RECAP

1 Identify your power influencers.

2 Identify the amplifiers who influence your power influencers.

3 Review your calendar from the last 90 days and reset it for maximum influence.

4 Evaluate your internal and external valuation; how is your valuation holding back your company growth?

5 Who else in your company needs to increase their valuation externally to improve the rapid growth of your company?

6 How Magnetic Are you? Missing, Mystery, Memorable or Magnetic?

7 What is one action you could take to increase your magnetism for the greatest business impact?

Endnotes

1 McNish, J and Silcoff, S (2016) *Losing the Signal: The untold story behind the extraordinary rise and spectacular fall of Blackberry*, Flatiron Books, New York

2 Bhutani, Ankita and Saha, Prasenjit (2019) Smart Refrigerator Market Report, *Global Market Insights*, https://www.gminsights.com/industry-analysis/smart-refrigerator-market?utm_source=GoogleAds&utm_medium=Adwords&utm_campaign=Electronics-PPC&gclid=CjwKCAiA1L_xB RA2EiwAgcLKA0IYi6FJNPVxAuUrsfpbk3Lr9smbY6BXgj1W-YIKW4WQqe4rjsJT-hoCyyoQAvD_BwE (archived at https://perma.cc/N55P-5LQJ)

3 Sabbagh, Dan and O'Neill, Sean (2001) Marconi: from boom to bust in a year, *The Daily Telegraph*, https://www.telegraph.co.uk/news/uknews/1339789/Marconi-from-boom-to-bust-in-a-year.html (archived at https://perma.cc/E7MW-YW77)

4 Dyson, James (2014) Yes, it's OK, it took me 5,127 attempts to make a bagless vacuum, *The Globe and Mail*, https://www.theglobeandmail.com/report-on-business/careers/leadership-lab/yes-its-ok-it-took-me-5127-attempts-to-make-a-bagless-vaccuum/article19992476 (archived at https://perma.cc/BGH3-A8BD)

CHAPTER TWO

Rapidly putting people in the right job for rapid growth

As I was completing my research for this book, there was a common theme that emerged from my observations and informal conversations with executives around the world: companies that grow faster than their competition have the right leaders at the top and leading each functional area. So before considering whether your business is rapidly growing in the right way, you must first determine if you and the rest of your organization are in the right job. Rapid growth in companies happens when the right leader, leadership team and creative, technical and business minds are in their perfect jobs. If you are already thinking that you are in your dream job, that is brilliant; read on and consider whether your team members are in their perfect jobs or what changes you need to make.

CHAPTER TOPICS

• What would be your perfect job?
• Three steps to defining your perfect job
• Five steps to finding your perfect job

A trend has evolved over the last couple of years: executives, leaders and experts are being tapped relentlessly by companies and headhunters. The era when decades of corporate service in one company was expected, rewarded and encouraged appears to be over. The era of a lifetime's service in one company only, rewarded by a carriage clock or gold watch on retirement, are no longer. In fact, many reading this might not even understand that reference, as a new normal of shorter stints at companies has started to emerge. To capitalize on this increasing mobility trend, you need to know how to define and find your perfect job.

There are hundreds of assessments available to evaluate yourself (some of them valid and some of them a lawsuit waiting to happen!), and there is a reason why these evaluations are so common: because people want to learn more about themselves. However, what these assessments will not do is take apart your job history, determine the components of your perfect job, and then assess just how well you are fitting into your perfect job today and what you need to do about it if you are not. You can start with the Triple E Assessment for Your Perfect Job and asking yourself some critical questions. (See Figure 2.1.)

What would be your perfect job?

Consider your own job today and examine the Triple E Assessment for Your Perfect Job:

• **Expertise**
  – Do you have the skills, knowledge and right personal tools to do your job?

- **Experience**
  - Do you have BTDTGR (Been There Done That Got Results)?
  - Does your background position you perfectly for your current role?
  - Is this the perfect culmination of your past positions?
- **Excitement**
  - Do you feel a thrill about your current role?
  - Do you willingly share with others the best parts of your role and do you feel lucky and honored to be in it?
  - Is your enthusiasm contagious?

If you possess the expertise and excitement for your role because you have the skills and knowledge required, but you don't have BTDTGR, you can still be successful with a strong support structure of mentors and coaching. However, you have to make sure you don't *fail to compete* either in your business or with your own personal career because you are in the biggest job of your life.

FIGURE 2.1 The Triple E Assessment

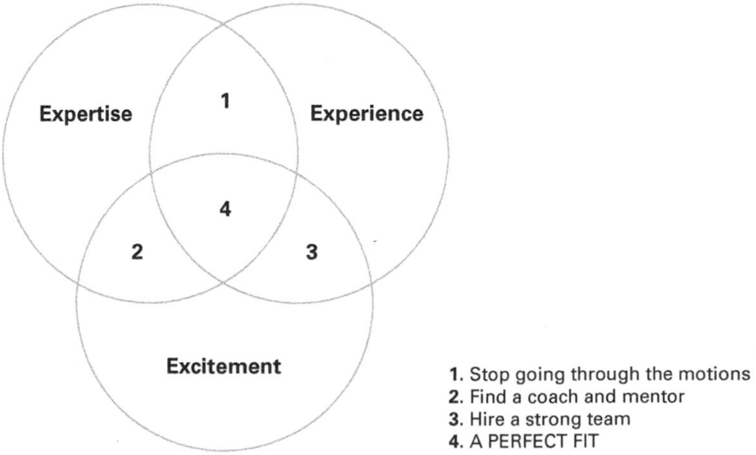
Expertise
Experience
Excitement
1
2
3
4
1. Stop going through the motions
2. Find a coach and mentor
3. Hire a strong team
4. A PERFECT FIT

If you have been there, done that and got results but you lack some skills and knowledge, focus fast on filling that gap. You can find ways to teach yourself or hire people for your team who do have that expertise. Both options can lead to success, but you need to act quickly.

Now, the third and final scenario is the highest risk and carries the biggest impact of all. If you have the perfect expertise and experience but lack excitement, then you are *going through the motions* and it is likely that you can feel it and so can everyone else around you. This is the worst possible scenario and the one that impacts growth the most. Just as stagnant water that sits in your garden for too long becomes repugnant, a person stagnant in their role can start to repel others. This is the greatest warning sign that you need to find a way to get excited again about your job, or find another role fast.

It's time to define what precisely would make your perfect job enviable. A little work and three easy steps will help you do just that.

Three steps to defining your perfect job

Step one: Discover what makes your eyes sparkle

One of my favorite questions for executives is asking them to think back to the job that they enjoyed most in their career. How about you? What is the job that you were really excited about, the one that you absolutely loved getting up for every day? What was it about that job that made it so fabulous – that you loved so much?

You may need time to reflect, but it's worth putting in the time to deconstruct it. Consider specifically the parts of the job that you enjoyed most. When you meet someone who really loves their job, their eyes sparkle. Their excitement is palpable. I was in Silicon Valley speaking to a group of chief information officers and I met someone from a well-known technology company who was incredibly excited and endlessly animated about his job. He was thrilled about what his team had achieved and how much empowerment he had. I asked him what specifically he enjoyed the most about his job, and he said, 'My boss and the board trust me to do what I say I am going to do and I do it, so everyone is happy.' Consider how simple that is – how valuable trust and empowerment are.

When you meet someone who really loves their job, their eyes sparkle.

Take a look in the mirror (yes, literally) and think about your current and previous roles and watch your face when you think and talk about your job. Now, some of you may be thinking what many people say to me, 'Hey Val, I've never really had a job that makes it sound like that.' I understand that, but there might be components of different jobs that you've had that make you feel that way. What aspects of previous roles make your eyes sparkle? Understanding that is a critical component of understanding what your perfect job might be.

Step two: Take a walk down memory lane

Now it's time to evaluate whether you have truly captured all of your past achievements. The best way to determine that is to find a quiet place and dust off all your past files, news clippings and electronic collections of your past roles, companies and work achievements. You might need to print off your resumé and literally go through each role to remember every project, initiative, acquisition, product launch, marketing event and detail. Yes, this is work, but it will be worth it.

Then ask yourself the blunt question: 'So what?' What was the impact on revenue, customers, costs, market share and profit? Don't forget to note what awards or recognition you achieved. Also consider what memorable events or launches you were involved in.

I recommend capturing those memories using whatever method works for you: a document, flipcharts, pictures, it's up to you. The idea is to create a Career Memory Lane walkthrough. A corporate real estate executive I was working with arrived at our one-on-one executive retreats with a stack of cartoons he had drawn to memorialize all of his past achievements. Drawing might not be your thing (it's not mine), but take some time to document all of it.

It often helps to work with someone else on this because you will likely gloss over an achievement, while someone else will see its importance. One executive casually mentioned to me how she had got a product on the top daytime US TV show *Ellen*, second only to Oprah in ratings. That kind of exposure and marketing is something that most CEOs would be desperate to achieve, but to her it wasn't significant until she heard someone else's reaction to it. Consider having a mentor or an executive peer you trust review your memories to extract the most significant results. You will be able to use these stories and snippets in interviews, and they provide great highlights for your resumé and media features.

Step three: Define your Perfect Job North Star

The Perfect Job North Star, shown in Figure 2.2, is a spider diagram, or a star with eight points, and on those eight points there are eight factors. Now you can have six, you can have ten, but what you want to do is identify the top factors that will determine your perfect job. You create the star by using your Career Memory Lane. Simply use the components, not the job itself. In addition, you have to think about other factors that reflect your desires and needs.

For some executives I work with, what is really important is that they get to travel around the world and have a lot of variety in the locations where they work. For them, lots of global travel has an incredibly high importance, and it should be a factor on

FIGURE 2.2 Your Perfect Job North Star

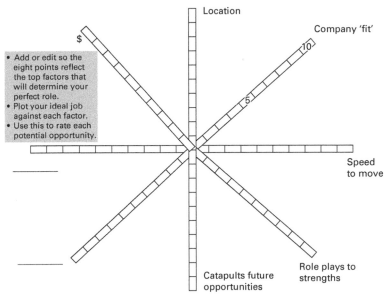

their Perfect Job North Star. I work with many executives in Los Angeles, and a sane commute is essential for them, because if you live in Manhattan Beach, you can't possibly get a job on the west side of Los Angeles without being willing to give up four hours of your day every day. For those executives, location is critical and would appear on their Perfect Job North Star. You may have immediately thought of several essential factors for your perfect job, but it's okay if you need to give it more thought. Go through and create your criteria to put on each point of your Perfect Job North Star. If you are struggling to figure out your perfect-job factors, you might want to consider this list:

1 empowerment;
2 commute;
3 amount of travel;
4 global responsibility;

5   specific industry;
6   P&L ownership;
7   location;
8   size of team;
9   remarkable boss;
10 external conference and media exposure;
11 exposure to CEO and board;
12 Growth-Maintenance-Disruption phase;
13 manageable workload;
14 company cause you care about;
15 marketable company name for the future;
16 chance to hire your own team;
17 $$ – compensation package;
18 pre-IPO;
19 one of first 20 employees;
20 uniquely positioned to leverage what you do best.

You might read the list and say yes to all 20 criteria, but some might be nice-to-haves, not must-haves. Pick your top eight and get on with finding that perfect job.

IDEAL COMPANY, IDEAL LOCATION

Two critical factors in determining your perfect job are physical location and the exact company or division you want to target. There are a couple of executives I'm working with at the moment who say things like this: 'I will only ever work in New York and I'll never leave.' But then, the next minute, they say, 'Well, I'm actually talking to a company about relocating to Silicon Valley because the company is my perfect company.' Head-spinning, right? They go from saying they will never leave to I will leave for these three companies. Sometimes they haven't even thought it through themselves, never mind talked about it with their significant others. This is the time to be really clear with yourself, and it may take some reflection. This isn't something that you're going to be able to decide in one conversation, especially if it involves a move to another state – or country. As you think this through, ask yourself:

- What is your perfect location?
- What is a possible location?
- What is a No Way! location?

Now do the same for your ideal companies:

- What is a perfect company?
- What is a possible company?
- Who is on your No Way! company list?

These could be specific company names, or industry segments, or types of companies. You might have a very fixed mindset and think you only want to work for start-ups, or you only want to work for Fortune 1000 companies, or that it's time to be an entrepreneur. Either way, you have to know what avenues you are considering and have an intentional outreach plan that is specific to you.

TURNING DOWN TWO JOBS FOR THE RIGHT REASONS
One executive, after completing the Perfect Job North Star, turned down two jobs that her mentors were telling her were perfect because she just could not put her finger on why she wasn't excited. Her identity has been kept confidential. Here is what she learned:

> I had two opportunities this summer and I ended up turning them both down. Using your Perfect Job North Star gave me the insight and words for why I did this. Previously, I couldn't explain it to my mentors; they would say, 'You're crazy, you must take that CMO role.' Once I saw your funnel, it helped me to understand that it was because I didn't spend enough time in the opportunities and possibilities stage. I was being pushed to meet the leadership team and board members. I also met their private equity people and I went through the whole process. Since I am highly introverted

that was exhausting and honestly it was such an energy-zapper as opposed to one that was inspiring and I knew it was just not right. As I read your chapter, I realized it's because I haven't really identified the top things that are important to me and mapped them to an industry, company or role. This was invaluable. Had I not read it I might have taken the job out of exhaustion at the thought of going through it all again for another opportunity. It would have been all for the wrong reasons and I would have been the reason the company didn't grow as fast as it could. I wasn't the right leader to lead that marketing function.

Triple reflection

It takes guts to turn down a job, and it takes even more confidence to fire yourself from your current job. Without the right leaders in place, you might experience rapid growth, but it will be done wrong, and you won't grow your company as fast as is possible. It is important not to just consider this for yourself, but also to think through how many of your direct team reporting to you are in their perfect job. Then ask them to cascade their assessment of their own teams until you have evaluated your whole company to determine whether people are in their perfect jobs, given the strategy and direction of your business.

> It takes guts to turn down a job, and it takes even more confidence to fire yourself from your current job.

Do you remember those Choose Your Own Adventure books? I loved them. I grew up in England, and my favorite cereal, Weetabix, had tokens you could collect to get free books. I loved the choice and ability to create my own story and move through the adventure at my own pace. I wanted to re-create that with this book: I do not want you to read this cover to cover; instead, choose your own adventure and skip between the chapters for rapid impact. Often you can read a book and get completely enthralled with the concepts and ideas but you really want to know HOW to implement a new idea. Throughout this book you will be getting the *what* and the *how* with tools that will help you get there faster. Here is a 'choose your own adventure' point: if you know you are not in the perfect job and want to know *how* to get there, we will go deeper now; or skip to Chapter 3 if you are already in your perfect job.

Five steps to finding your perfect job

If you know that you are not in your perfect job, here are the guidance, tools and advice that I give my executive clients when I am working with them on a career transition. I am no head-hunter, but I have unique experience from both sides of the table, inside and outside of corporate life. I have interviewed tens of thousands of people in my corporate career, and that's no exaggeration (I can explain the calculation for anyone curious). In my consulting practice, my clients move internally, get promoted and often move to other companies at that perfect time when their external valuation is higher than their internal personal valuation, as explained in Chapter 1.

You might have jumped here knowing that you need to find your next perfect job, or you might be starting to realize it is a possibility, or you could be in the middle of your job search with a couple of offers on the table. Before we get started with the advice, it will help to know where you are on the Career Transition Funnel (see Figure 2.3).

The Career Transition Funnel moves from entertaining opportunities to exploring possibilities to narrowing choices and then filtering decisions before you decide and then make it happen. What I see, however, is that executives often don't stay high enough in their funnel for long enough to make the most of their next career leap. Where are you?

FIGURE 2.3 Career Transition Funnel

An executive who had heard me speak at a conference the previous year called me and said, 'Val, my company was acquired last month and I couldn't tell you about it until now. It was only announced last week.' I remembered he had been there for over a decade and said to him, 'That's brilliant news. What a great time to consider what is next for you and get rid of your two-hour daily commute.' There was a long pause before he replied, 'Yes. I was really worried because I was unsure about how long I was going to be out of the workforce so I've already accepted another job. It's a great job. It's maybe a bit more of a drive, but it's with someone I've worked with in the past.'

He'd leapt right into a decision, before lighting up his network, considering possibilities and probably without truly taking time to reflect on what he loved to do and what his next perfect job would be. He missed every single step of the Career Transition Funnel and went straight to decision. Now it could be that this was the perfect job for him and that he was going to be delighted and happy. But he missed out on discovering his market worth. He made a commitment before learning about other opportunities that were available to him. And 99.9 per cent of his network had no idea he was even on the market or looking. This story could have ended with him living happily ever after in this new job. But he missed out.

I see this time and time again: people respond to headhunter calls or to an offer right in front of them, rather than truly managing their next career transition. To make the most of opportunities, you want to consider the top of the funnel before you jump to a decision.

Here's what each step means for you and what you need to do at each phase.

Step one: Entertaining opportunities

Before you start considering any opportunities, complete an online search of yourself. This matters because this is exactly what executives, board members and hiring managers do before meeting you, accepting your call or replying to your email. They want to know: *who are you?* The essential elements of your magnetism should be on clear display. Does the virtual you match the real you?

Does the virtual you match the real you?

Take five minutes now to put your browser in private browser mode and complete an online search of your name. The private browser mode allows you to see what others see rather than being influenced by your past search history. The first question to answer is this: can you even find yourself? If you have a common name, you might be confused with many others. If you can find yourself, what do the results say about you? Do they fully reflect your brilliance and achievements? Does the virtual you reflect who you are and what you want to be known for?

There is no doubt that when you are going through the recruitment process, board members, executives and the people who will interview you will be completing online searches on you – perhaps even 15 minutes prior to the interview. That's what used to happen when I was on the corporate side, interviewing hundreds of executives each year. I'd complete a quick online search to find out who they were. I would listen to videos of them speaking at conferences, hear their points of views in media interviews, or look at how they were featured in articles.

This is a critical way you can move up the 'magnetically brilliant executive ladder' covered in Chapter 1. The more online content about you that fits who you are as a leader and what you want to be known for, the more you will increase your magnetism, so others will be compelled to follow you and want to learn more, and even possibly work for you!

If you are not satisfied with what you see, hold back and fix it first before waking up your network, because you will not get the credit for your brilliance when your long-lost colleagues search online for who you are and what you have achieved.

When you are satisfied that the virtual you appropriately reflects the real you, it is time for your Leadership Landscape Look. This is where you want to scan your landscape in the broadest sense of what is possible. Depending on your strength as a Magnetic Executive, this may be hard work or incredibly easy. This is the point when many executives realize just how little positive magnetism they naturally create. You want to light up your network and make sure everyone who knows you is aware that you are looking and what your perfect role could look like. This is where you need to quickly understand what creates your magnetic draw in creative, technical and business minds.

Consider reflecting on your experience by using Table 2.1.

Too often creative leaders will talk about their achievements through the lens of what is important for their creative minds and creative colleagues. They may not use language that describes the business benefits or the technical achievements from their work. When Creative Director Shane Small launched the highest-backed Kickstarter in history, raising $8,782,571 with 219,382 backers, he couldn't help but point to the business impact of his

TABLE 2.1 Innovation Trifecta of Achievements

	ACHIEVEMENT 1	ACHIEVEMENT 2	ACHIEVEMENT 3
Creative Results			
Technical Results			
Business Results			

creativity. Sometimes, however, it takes more thought and reflection to make the business connection of creative input.

'I really don't know how to think about my proudest achievements,' is something I often hear from leaders considering the matter for the first time. I did this exercise at an executive conference in England recently. A CEO said to me: 'I'm running a technology company. It's my own business. I've grown it. I have 600 people working for me, and we've been profitable for the last eight years. I just don't know what to talk about in terms of my proudest achievements.' In response, I said, 'Well, let's start there. There are some really great achievements in how you have built your business.' We unpacked his business's impact and success, which extended far beyond his revenue and profit growth.

I spoke with another executive at the same event who said, 'I really don't know how to think about this because I have spent a lot of my time in the non-profit world, and I created this foundation, and I dedicate most of my weekends to this foundation. It's one supporting disadvantaged youth.' Again, she was telling me the story and, as she did, she looked at me and said, 'That's one of my achievements, isn't it?' Sometimes, it takes a conversation. You need somebody sitting next to you, which is why it is helpful to have a circle of advisors, who can give you guidance and help you talk this through. Think of some people who know you well and can help extract it from you; they will help you identify your proudest achievements and how they impact the creative, technical and business aspects of your company.

IS YOUR NETWORK NEGLECTED?

You don't just need your network when you are looking for your next job; strategic partnerships, seeking new investors, hiring new board members or trying to attract new sponsors all rely on the strength of your network. Yours may need a nudge, a poke or a vigorous shake depending on how you have been tending to it over the last five years. If you have a desolate network of people around you, start today by looking over your network and asking for introductions to people you want to meet. It will take longer, but you need to update your network at some point, and many people find job-hunting just about the only time they prioritize contacting and maintaining their network. Your incentive is feeling the pain of a neglected network; I find that once this happens, no leader ever lets their network become desolate again.

These are some powerful conversation starters:

- *Say to people who could hire you*: 'After launching ____ initiative I'm now considering what is next. I would love some advice.'
- *Say to people who know people who could hire you*: 'I've worked on __, ____, and ____ products in the last few years. I'd love some advice about who to talk to as I consider what is next for me.'

There is a US tradition that I don't think has spread widely to the rest of the world. In the United States many people send Christmas holiday letters that are a review of their year gone by. Some are lengthy picture books of holidays or kids' achievements, some are stories with candid lessons and insights. While some might find this personal sharing a little over the top and braggadocio behavior, it can be translated to your business life and help you, whether you are looking for your perfect job or helping your team move on and find their perfect job outside of the team. The good news is that you don't have to wait until the end of the year to do it. Consider writing a recap of your work life, future opportunities and where you are looking for advice or recommendations. It is a unique way to do a quick

Consider writing a recap of your work life, future opportunities and where you are looking for advice or recommendations.

update for those whom you may not have spoken to for a while or those who do not know of your current brilliance and achievements. It's an easy way to keep your network up to date.

RAPID GROWTH ACCELERATOR TIP: VALUABLE VIDEO REQUEST

I'll share one tip that I usually only disclose to my executive clients; only those who really want to see fast results from their network actually follow through and do it. It will take you just 10 minutes, and you will absolutely get a faster, more interested response from those you know or don't know. Here's how you do it rapidly:

1 Grab your phone.
2 Sit with natural light landing on your face and hold your phone at eye level or slightly above.
3 Press record.
4 In 90 seconds record three sentences: who you are and your last achievement; what you are looking for next; a request for advice.
   – Here's an example from a leader I worked with:
     – My name is Tara Moeller and I most recently was interim general manager and Head of Marketing at CamelBak, where we launched a new direct-to-consumer platform internationally and created two new categories during challenging market times.
     – I'm now considering CMO, divisional president and board opportunities with innovative fast-growing companies.
     – I'd love your advice on companies I should be talking to before I make my final decision on my next opportunity.
5 Now save it using a private link on Vimeo/YouTube/Dropbox.
6 Then send that private link out to everyone you know.

This will get attention more than another text, voicemail or email, and it gives you a chance to personalize the message as if you were sitting across from someone, having a cup of coffee or a chat at a meeting.

Step two: Evaluate possibilities

Once you have awakened your network, you will start to get enquiries and have choices to make. This can be a lonely time for executives. It can be challenging to be employed while navigating opportunities without your current company or boss finding out too soon, yet needing advice now more than ever. This is where you tap into your enviable inner circle. Share your Perfect Job North Star with them, prepare for conversations, debrief interviews and test whether you are evaluating all of your options objectively. This is where some executives hire an expert to guide them through the transition. This is a small part of my business; I work one-on-one with some executives as their navigator through this complex process, which seems to vary from company to company.

I'll dispel one myth that often surprises leaders: you have to ignore all recruiters and headhunters. I realize this sounds counterintuitive. You might even think I'm crazy. But the biggest mistake people make is chasing recruiters and headhunters. I know because I've been inside organizations like Microsoft, Amazon, BMW and House of Fraser. I know what happens inside recruitment teams. The fastest way you can get yourself in front of your ideal company is by ignoring the recruiters and going straight to the executives who make the decisions.

> *I'll dispel one myth that often surprises leaders: you have to ignore all recruiters and headhunters.*

Because the executives who make the decisions are going to know far more about the person that they're trying to hire than the recruiters are.

I know some really fantastic recruiters, but even the most fabulous recruiters do not understand every job and the possibilities. Executives have the power to create a job that hasn't even been thought of yet. That is your ideal situation. What's better than being able to say, 'Well, I know you're looking for a VP of sales, but my expertise is really in digital expansion. So how about we create a job where we combine digital expansion and sales?' That actually happened with one of my clients earlier this year.

This is why considering your perfect job criteria is important. Rather than describing your perfect job in very specific terms when an executive asks you what you want to do next, you can say something like: 'I would like to be able to build and grow my own team. I would like to be empowered to be able to make strategic product decisions.' Talk about the critical factors and then be open to exploring what is possible.

This is why you want to talk to executives, not recruiters, because recruiters usually only know about the approved, open roles that they currently have on their desks in front of them. The good, strategic recruiters might know about future opportunities, too, and the absolutely brilliant ones may be in lockstep with the CEO and fully understand their business strategy and what they're trying to do in three years' time, but those people are few and far between. That's why you want to talk to executives, because they can talk about future possibilities. You can talk about what you can bring, and then they can potentially create a job for you. Or, if there isn't something right now, they can keep you in mind or refer you to that friend who works for the other technology company down the road. This is why thinking about how you can prepare for and answer questions is also key.

Of course, you may come across your perfect job that is solely represented by a headhunter, but even then your aim is to get in front of the hiring executives as soon as possible.

I assure you this effort will pay off. If you truly want to find your perfect job, it helps to think about your life in chapters. Your current chapter affects what you may want to do. You may be in an experimental chapter where you want to quit your corporate job, launch a start-up, give back to a non-profit, or tour the world. You may be in a very different position now than where you want to be. This increases the importance of how you position yourself externally to set yourself up best for success.

If you're at the point where you're feeling ready to move out of your corporate life, start doing advisory work, sit on a few boards and speak at events – essentially re-create what your work life looks like – that's going to require a different focus. If you are in a company and you're ready to move to a bigger company or you want to go to a private company, again, each of these factors will determine how you position yourself externally. Everyone's evaluation cycle is different, but the key is to be intentional and deliberate.

Step three: Choices

Because of the work you have already put in with your Perfect Job North Star, this part comes a lot easier. You can chart each of your opportunities and score them against your criteria. It is far easier to make choices when you have a defined set of criteria to measure them against. The most challenging part of this step is aligning every opportunity to land at around the right time. Ideally, you will have at least two job offers in front of you at precisely the same time. To achieve that you might have to speed up some opportunities and slow down others, which you can achieve by how available you are to attend interviews and follow-up meetings.

Step four: Decision time!

Most people leave money on the table when it is decision time. I know some of the best chief financial officers and business leaders who are incredible at business negotiation yet abysmal at negotiating their own personal job offer or contract. Consider the 'rule of three no's' when negotiating your compensation package: if you haven't been told no three times, there is still room to increase your offer! Aside from the usual base salary, bonus and stock allocations, consider asking for sign-on bonuses, extra vacations, support for executive education, membership of executive communities, support of an executive advisor, agreement to lots of or no global travel, a future review date in writing for your compensation, or a change of control clause. These are just a few of the most overlooked additional bargaining incentives. If they keep saying yes, keep asking until they say no three times.

ASK VAL ANYTHING! FREE ADVICE

At this point you have now done a lot of research, reflection and thinking. You have hopefully talked with the mentors in your life – your coaches and advisors – and received many opinions and a lot of feedback. These are the steps that many people skip because they are reacting to the headhunter call, but you have taken a thoughtful approach. You have an idea now about what is ideal for you. You may be ready to start making decisions, and sometimes you need an impartial sounding board.

As a bonus feature for purchasing this book, you can ask me five complimentary questions via text. Go to www.textvalnow. com, enter your mobile phone number from anywhere in the world, and you will get an automatic text back from me. Tell me you bought this book, and then you can ask me any five questions about rapid growth done right that arises from reading this book. Ask me anything – I can't wait to help you.

Step five: GO!

This is the time when you launch into your perfect role. We will explore the scenario of starting a new role throughout Chapters 5 and 6 and how you set up your relationships for the most rapid success.

Don't procrastinate

When it comes to finding your perfect next job, the key is to make time for this before you really need it. Pick a time that is easy for you to dedicate to the steps we've examined. You can set aside 30 minutes, or you can set aside 15 minutes. Whatever it is, pick a consistent chunk of time (yes, even a 15-minute chunk!) and then open up your calendar and block it in right now. Schedule the next time when you are going to dedicate time to investing in evaluating your own perfect job and that of your team.

CHAPTER 2 RAPID RECAP

1 You need the right expertise, experience and excitement to drive rapid growth.

2 Ultimate bravery is saying no to a job offer or firing yourself because you won't grow in the right way.

3 The strength of your network will accelerate your board expertise, partnership opportunities, investment offers and your career.

4 Failing to put the right people in place means you will grow the wrong way.

5 To creatively capture and ask for advice from your network, record a video.

6 Be clear what makes your eyes sparkle in the work you do.

7 How does your immediate leadership team capture their individual and collective achievements?

8 State the creative, technical and business benefits of your results.

9 If you talk alone in a cave, you will only hear your own echo.

10 Evaluate quickly where you need to take action to have the right people in your perfect job.

CHAPTER THREE

Translating so you can speak creative, technical and business language fluently

'They just don't understand, Val!' is one of the most common observations I get whether I am working with marketing, engineering, finance, creative or technical-minded executives. They are talking about their colleagues, board members, peers and bosses. They say to me things like: 'If only the technical team would understand how we need to build a business model that will disrupt our industry'; 'If only the creative team would realize their ideas are technically impossible' or 'If only the business team would realize there will be no sustainable profit unless we have a creative experience that our customers love.'

CHAPTER TOPICS
- The Innovation Trifecta
- Increasing your trilingual power

- When translation fails
- Defrosting the feedback freeze
- The leadership insulation layer

Language matters – it is our vehicle for creating understanding. In business, however, many people feel as if they're trying to talk with alien life-forms when they're trying to work together. Creative, technical and business minds have long suffered the pain of being misunderstood, making a translator seem necessary at times. Through interviews with senior executives across insurance, sports, technology and education sectors, we will explore practical ways to discover the Rosetta Stone so you can crack the code to speaking a common language and driving innovation success. By the end of this chapter, you will be a trilingual executive, able to speak the language of technology, creativity and business.

I remember a particular meeting that illustrates what happens when people fail to find a common language. The view from the executive conference room was spectacular, the sun was setting and the sky was an array of red, orange and pink colors that distracted nearly everyone. A glass-eyed stare came from every executive in the room apart from one. The presenter had lost his audience ten minutes into a thirty-minute discussion. He either didn't notice, or did notice but didn't know what to do. I know that he cared, because before the meeting he told me just how important the meeting was to him. The chief technology officer was discussing the strategic choices for the executive team. There were critical decisions that needed to be made to determine what investments needed to take place, he needed the support of everyone around the table, but he had lost their attention to the sunset.

The backdrop might not always be a beautiful sunset, but I have seen this scene play out over a hundred times in conversations around the world. This chapter deconstructs exactly why that happens and what to do to prevent it, correct it and ensure that you can effectively translate the message you need to present across the technical-, creative- and business-minded people you work with.

When I was working for European telecommunications giant Marconi in the late nineties, the region I covered included Italy and Germany where we had large regional offices for our technical network operating centers. While I had traveled to both countries as a tourist, arriving to do business in a foreign country required a greater understanding of the language, so I started taking weekly Italian lessons. Although English was the company's common business language, I knew there would be many moments when I wanted to understand the casual conversations in between meetings and the inside jokes. I noticed that the executives who had mastered the local language, or were attempting to master it, had greater respect, influence and support from the local teams.

At Marconi we entered into a joint venture with the British biotech company Oxford Glycosciences to map the human genome. They provided the creative ideas and science, and we at Marconi provided the technology and data storage under a new company Confirmant. When you travel to a foreign country, you get a guide or learn critical phrases of the local language so that you can survive. The same applies in business – creative, technical and business people need a guide – a Rosetta Stone – to help them to understand each other.

The Innovation Trifecta

The most common trait of companies that can break the mold with new ideas is an ability to create a symbiotic relationship

FIGURE 3.1 The Innovation Trifecta symbiosis

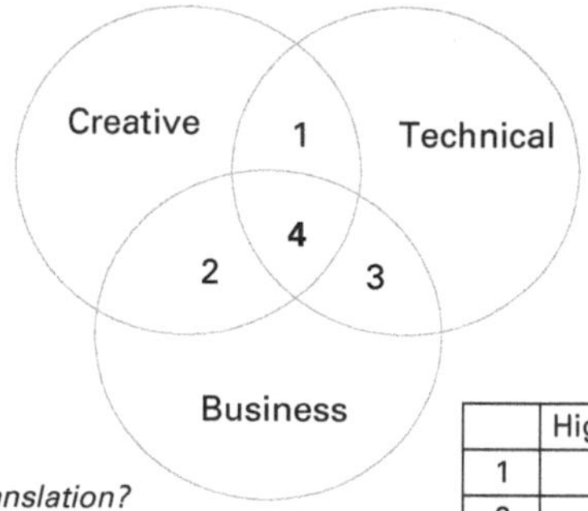

Where is your strength?
Where is your friction?
Where are you lost in translation?
Where do you have goal alignment?

	High / Medium / Low
1	
2	
3	
4	

between creative, technical and business minds. When I coach executives and their teams, I call this the Innovation Trifecta; it is what occurs when there is a mutually beneficial connection between very different parts of your business. With this in place, you'll unleash the power of innovation within your company and create innovative products and services that your customers will love.

Now consider the strength of your symbiosis across your creative, technical and business teams. Using Figure 3.1 rate how strong your symbiosis is – high, medium or low. This creates a snapshot and shows you where you have work to do. This chapter and Chapter 5 provide the tools you can use to improve those relationships to create rapid growth.

Your Innovation Trifecta in action

Here are three ways to tell if you are unleashing this power within your company:

1 **Complement your CEO's expertise**
   First, consider your CEO: are they deeply technical, is their expertise creative, or do they perhaps have a business background? You have to start by understanding and noting the

power of your CEO, then assess if they have complementary talents on their executive team and board. Like the sun in the solar system, the expertise of your CEO is the pivotal power of your organization, and the rest of your leadership team need complementary talents that orbit the CEO like planets. Jeff Bezos has a precision-sharp business brain and he knows how to surround himself with genius technical talent. Amazon is swarming with the best technical brains on the planet. Does your CEO have mini-me's around them who just repeat what they say or a complementary set of minds?

Like the sun in the solar system, the expertise of your CEO is the pivotal power of your organization.

2 **Identify your weakest link**
   Consider using Figure 3.1 to review the capability and capacity of your technical, creative and business talent. Do you have the expertise, availability and experience needed to deliver your business results? If not, you are holding back the power of your potential rapid growth and your ability to innovate. You need to create a shared understanding of where your strengths are and where your weakest link lies. When I was working on the Amazon Fashion leadership team as part of transforming the Amazon Fashion experience, we knew as a leadership team that we had to strengthen our creative expertise. Disruptive creative marketing was unheard of in 2011 at Amazon because their focus was mainly on books and basics, so as a leadership team we had to break the company mold and go and hire the best industry talent that would bring a creative expertise to drive the changes we needed to capture a significant share of the $500 billion fashion industry. Where do you have strength and where is your weakest link – with your creative, technical or business expertise?

3 **Replicate the Shrimp and Goby Effect**
   A pistol shrimp is nearly blind. It cannot see when its predators are nearby and wouldn't last long if it didn't create a symbiotic

relationship with the watchman goby. When we had a marine aquarium, these were our favorite two inhabitants because we could observe two very unlikely creatures working together for mutual benefit. The pistol shrimp uses its large claws to dig caves for the watchman goby, and the goby keeps the shrimp safe from predators. Companies need to build similar symbiotic relationships between creative, technical and business minds. Too often companies operate as if they have landed in Japan but are trying to speak French. What is getting lost in translation in your company?

I am rarely surprised at conferences, but I will never forget a talk I heard at Evanta's CIO conference in Los Angeles in 2018. It was an unusual double act. Both the chief information officer and the chief marketing officer from Farmers Insurance were presenting. What made this unusual was the fact that they were presenting together like a perfect comedy duo, finishing each other's sentences and being incredibly candid as they shared the lessons learned from a successful digital transformation that crossed both the marketing and technology strategy, with a significant impact on the business's success. This was a perfect example of the Innovation Trifecta at work: leaders had come together and formed a dynamic partnership – so strong that a marketing executive was comfortable standing on stage at a technology conference with his partner in innovation and jointly sharing stories of success that transformed how customers accessed their insurance services.

Increasing your trilingual power

How are you creating symbiotic relationships across your creative, technical and business teams? It starts with learning how to become a 'trilingual executive'. Companies that are too focused and heavy on technical expertise will lose creativity. Those that are too creative may not have a profitable solution. Companies that weight decisions purely on business metrics won't delight customers and create exponential growth through innovation. Balance and symbiosis are the name of the game.

Once you have determined the strength of your Innovation Trifecta in your business, then and only then is it time to assess how trilingual you are and build a plan to create rapid growth by increasing your trilingual power. You can start with the following assessment. (See Figure 3.2.)

The trilingual executive assessment

Rate yourself using a scale of 1–10, with 10 being the highest, for each of the crucial elements and essential behaviors of a trilingual executive.

FIGURE 3.2 The trilingual executive assessment

Crucial elements   *Rate yourself*

- Sets goals
- Dedicates open space for exploration
- Provides frequent feedback   _____
- Creates spontaneous glue   **10**
- Maintains broad perspective

Essential behaviors

- Curious questioner
- Endless empathy
- Publicly vulnerable   _____
- Perpetual learner   **10**
- Ultimate translator

Rapid Growth!

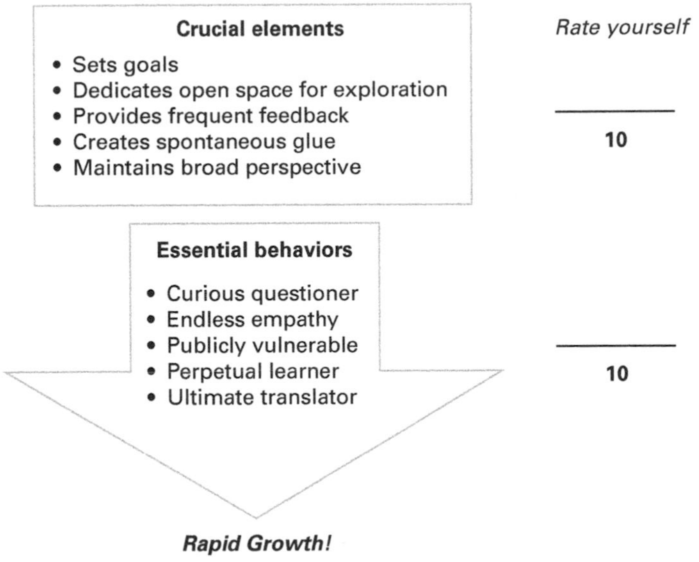

THE FIVE CHARACTERISTICS OF A TRILINGUAL EXECUTIVE

- **Goal-oriented**
  A trilingual executive requests input into goals from creative, technical and business peers. To become a truly trilingual executive you have to start with how you create your goals. Too often I see these created in silos, when a simple step of asking for input prior to creation would allow you to unlock faster growth.

- **Values white space freedom**
  A trilingual executive dedicates time to open-space exploration of future possibilities with creative, technical and business teams. Chapter 7 provides ideas on exactly how you do this.

- **Feedback provider**
  A trilingual executive provides frequent and fast feedback beyond their own team and discipline. At the end of this chapter we explore this further.

- **Connective**
  A trilingual executive creates spontaneous glue between functions.

- **Maintains a broad perspective**
  A trilingual executive sources insights from customers and the outside world. Creating bold challenges accelerates these perspectives. Online real-estate company Zillow launched a $1 million prize for anyone who could work out how to improve the accuracy of one of its algorithms that predicts home values. Teams of data scientists around the world competed for the prize, broadening the brain power of new machine-learning techniques that an internal team alone could never have mastered.

THE FIVE ESSENTIAL BEHAVIORS OF A TRILINGUAL EXECUTIVE

A trilingual executive does the following:

1 **Asks questions.** A trilingual executive seeks to understand differences. When you are a tourist abroad, you have to ask

the right questions to avoid misinterpreting the local language. Business is no different. Knowing the right question to ask is an essential component to understanding your peers who are different from you.

2 **Provides empathy.** Ronalee Zarate-Bayani, CMO of the Los Angeles Rams, shared with me: 'The reason there has been a trend in the last five years to hire executives in from other industries is to bring in a new perspective because they need to disrupt their existing model, but what tends to happen is, in order to be successful, a lot of executives have to curtail or curb that difference in order to move the needle from within the company. That is where you have to be empathetic, but still authentic to who you are. The fact that my last seven jobs didn't exist, the fact that I was able to create, build, transform from scratch in terms of having a vision and then building it out, be it changing things or working cross-functionally to make it happen, the common theme for success has always been about doing things differently and opening the aperture of perspective for the organization. You have to be empathetic with your peers in other functions to achieve that.'

A trilingual executive transports themselves into others' shoes with kindness. At my daughters' convocation, the Head of Westridge School for Girls, Elizabeth McGregor, embraced empathy as the theme for the 2019–2020 school year. The need for empathy extends far beyond the school playground and classroom, though it is often associated with childlike undertones. Empathy usually involves comparisons. Sure you feel a little for your new technology leader who has just joined the company, but if only they knew how hard YOU had it when you joined – it was far worse. You might not say it out loud, but it is common to have such thoughts. That new sales leader completely missed the mark on their portion of the sales kickoff presentation; she wasn't prepared, but you are managing three acquisitions in parallel and you managed to prepare well, so why can't she? Of course your board presentation was too long and they said you had too many slides and too much detail, but they need to learn to consume more information and get used to this level of detail. Although we sometimes think we are being empathetic, there are often 'buts' attached to it. Every one of those real quotes from leaders above has a BUT in it, which disqualifies any ounce of true empathy. It also doesn't allow you to fully jump into the life and mind of the person you are trying to extend empathy towards. Our barriers to empathy usually arise when we are reminded of something in ourselves. We criticize those unable to be concise because we fear we may be too verbose ourselves, or we point out others' inability to launch a successful product because we are still reeling from our past disastrous product launch. At first you may not realize just why you are lacking empathy, or you may not have stopped to listen to your judgmental views on others, but it's zapping your energy, taking up too much of your mental spin cycle, and holding you back from unlocking deeper connections and relationships with others.

Although we sometimes think we are being empathetic, there are often 'buts' attached to it.

3   **Displays vulnerability.** A trilingual executive shares stories of success and failure. Successes are easy to share, but it is also important to be able to learn from and share stories about the times you haven't achieved the results you are looking for. This helps unlock growth, as others learn the creative, technological or business impacts from your candid stories about when things didn't go as planned.

4   **Perpetual learner.** The trilingual executive continually seeks to improve their level of knowledge. Mark Essayian, president of IT Services company KME Systems, knows how to be a perpetual learner. He went to school to become a nuclear physicist, because he truly wanted to know why the sky was blue. His father was a nuclear atomic engineer who

worked on the Nevada Test Site. He instilled such a sense of curiosity in Mark that he has a constant thirst for learning, whether it is fixing a car, finding out how electricity works, or how the creative marketing experts learn how to influence buying behavior. I was most curious about how Mark instils this thirst for learning in others. Here is what he shared with me: 'First you have to make it fun and interesting. I became a teaching assistant because my faculty advisor said, "Do this and take that load off my back or I won't let you graduate," and I learned really quickly that if you don't make it fun and interesting at the same time, people just close off, their eyes will glaze over and they'll just look at the book and start drawing something. So I always struggled to give these real-world examples, which was tough in the field when I started doing more advanced physics and math. But those people were there to learn, and they were there to understand what that concept was. I did my best to keep them engaged. If you have someone engaged, then give them the information. Now it is easy in the work I do supporting companies with their IT systems. There is always a reason to learn new technology, new marketing techniques or new ways to make money.'

5 **Translates context.** The trilingual executive provides relevant explanations in context. While running a leadership workshop, Jennifer Anaya, SVP of Marketing for Ingram Micro, shared with her leaders her expectations for how she wanted them to lead: 'I need you to be the translator who takes our marketing programs and initiatives and explains them using metrics that each of your functional groups care about. Use language and metrics that matter to them.' Being such a translator is a pivotal accelerator in achieving alignment and shared understanding that will pull together those who think differently towards collective rapid growth.

Now that you have completed your Trilingual Assessment you have a greater understanding of what your strengths are and where you have opportunities for growth. Use the following tips to further accelerate your understanding of your creative, technical and business peers. Just as I took Italian lessons to help myself understand my Italian peers (and to be able to order a balanced meal), you can take lessons to increase your understanding and achieve better communication with those who don't share your mindset. This will help you achieve the ultimate goal of becoming trilingual.

Five ways to increase your business understanding

1 Immerse yourself in the business metrics that your company or division reports on. Create a glossary for your team of metrics that matter to your CEO and leadership team.
2 Read your annual report, earnings report, S1 filing or quarterly financial updates. Ask your finance leader to check your understanding or to answer questions you have.
3 For every single business and personal goal, extrapolate a financial impact. Connect your work to revenue, profit, market share and customer metrics that have a dollar sign. This exercise alone will help you attract the right attention when you are seeking to influence investment or prioritize decisions.
4 Watch CNBC's *Squawk Box* each morning and take note of the global, industry and competitive news stories. Also pay attention to the executives interviewed and observe how they frame their soundbites and answers so that listeners can rapidly absorb their message.
5 Go back to the floor and shadow every key function, including customer support, supply chain, sales, finance, operations, marketing and so forth, and identify where there are profit, revenue and efficiency gains.

If you follow each of these five ideas, you will set the context for your work and be able to answer what I call the 'so what?' question, which is: 'So what is the point of your work if you cannot frame it in business outcomes?' Master this and you will transform how your message is understood and acted upon.

Now you have grounded your understanding of the business element of becoming trilingual, let's look at how you can unlock your understanding and improve relationships with your creatively minded colleagues.

Five ways to embrace your creative understanding

1 Experiment with new ways of working to wake up your creative brain. Ewan Pidgeon, director of Creative Services at Ingram Micro, will regularly tell his peers to write with a different pen, sit at a different desk, take a different route to work or embrace other different habits to wake up their inner creativity. Doing so will help you experience what your creative peers do each day.

Experiment with new ways of working to wake up your creative brain.

2 Immerse yourself in the brand, design and user interface of your products and those of your competitors. Form opinions about what you experience and discuss it with your creative peers. Ever wondered why your logo is designed the way it is, or why the website landing page navigates the way it does? Everything is done for a reason and the more curious you can be, the more it will help you start to see how a creative mind works. This will accelerate your ability to speak to and gain the support of your creatively minded colleagues.

3 Shadow a creative colleague. Chris Capossela, chief marketing officer of Microsoft, regularly shares on his social-media channels pictures of himself being shadowed by engineering leaders. This helps set context, and lets you see the depth of thinking that goes into a creative brief. In the future, when you want to change or challenge an idea, you can practice your empathy for the work that came before it and the work that you will be triggering afterwards.

4 Attend a marketing event where industry experts are showcasing their work and ask your marketing colleagues what could be relevant for you. Perhaps you can take inspiration from the Farmers Insurance duo and even present together on stage.

5 Follow creative gurus. One of my favorites is Bonin Bough, one of the youngest C-suite executives who was behind the first-ever 3D printed food product, a customized Oreo. Bough now shares his brilliance through TV shows and his social-media channels. He is perfect for bursting your usual bubble of voices to listen to.

Once you have awakened new creative juices and understanding, you can then focus on how to embrace your inner technical genius.

Five ways to increase your technical prowess

In my work with leaders of all disciplines, this is the area I hear the greatest resistance to because of the fear of intricate details. Technology has become more complex, and the grandiose promises of artificial intelligence, machine learning and advanced robotics can overwhelm even the most technically curious. Here's how to overcome that fast:

1 Ask for a metaphor when a technology genius is giving an explanation. 'It is like someone changed the locks to our house and only they have the master key' is how a chief information security officer explained a highly complex situation for me. Before then he spent far too long giving me the intricacies of the security breach, which simply went over my head.

2 A picture explains a thousand technologies. Sometimes you just need a drawing, so ask for a visual representation of how all of your systems talk to each other, or how they are disconnected. Stand together in front of a whiteboard with a technology peer and draw it out together and it will help you see the dependencies and opportunities for how your work may become symbiotic.

3 Find a technical mentor. You don't want to be in a board meeting or an important customer meeting asking how one system works or what a particular company buzz word means. Identify a technical expert who can be your mentor on technology areas and whom you can feel free to ask any questions.

4 Sit in on a technical product design review or product development meeting so you can hear the language they use, or the areas they are debating. You might figure out a way your two teams could work together to solve a mutual challenge.

5 Shadow your technical peers. Put your endless empathy into practice. There is no better way to appreciate another colleague's life than to literally walk in their shoes for a day. Ask them for a day that would give you the most insight and increase your understanding of their world.

Now you have found ways to increase your business, creative and technical understanding, it is important to realize you won't always get it right, and sometimes translation fails.

When translation fails

Not long after getting engaged, my then fiancé and I took a trip to Milan. We delighted in the walking tours, shopping and restaurants. One night we decided to be adventurous and try a quaint-looking restaurant. This was before I had taken up Italian lessons, so when the menu was presented to us, I am sure the waiter was quietly amused at our look of sheer horror at the descriptions. We had a brief moment of panic because nothing looked familiar, and there was not a *pollo* in sight or a waiter who could speak English. So we decided to take a risk and with pointing and nervous smiles we placed our orders. When the waiter joyfully presented us with our dishes we received a humungous plate of asparagus, a plate with one fried egg in the centre, and an unknown green vegetable sautéed in a lake of melted butter. Our British politeness overtook us, and we smiled, said 'grazie', and ate what we had ordered.

Tailoring your message

Sometimes what you intend to say will get lost in translation. To overcome this, you have to be willing to spot it, seek to understand how you misspoke and rapidly correct it. Otherwise it can cost you millions of dollars and you won't deliver the products, services or results you expect to. This is where rapid growth can go wrong, so let's explore how to reduce the probability of that happening and how to fix it if you are lost in translation and misunderstood.

Defrosting the feedback freeze

Some leaders create a freeze on feedback, often without being aware of it. Take the Feedback Freeze Assessment to see where you fall:

1 I receive both positive and critical feedback on my ideas.
2 If someone external was to gather feedback on me, I could predict who would say what.
3 When I receive feedback, I am curious to learn more and always ask clarifying questions.
4 I always thank people for giving me feedback, even if I don't like what I am hearing.
5 My company encourages feedback and rewards candid feedback.
6 I frequently request feedback at pivotal moments in projects or initiatives.
7 When hiring, I question whether new employees will be open to frequent candid feedback.
8 I know when not to ask for feedback.

9 I correctly evaluate when to ignore, accept or park feedback.

10 I don't take feedback personally, but objectively seek to understand and evaluate it.

If you answered yes to eight or more questions, you have a healthy approach to feedback that will prevent you getting lost in translation and being misunderstood. If you achieved a score of less than five, take time to understand what you can do to defrost the areas that are freezing your ability to ask for, accept and apply the lessons that feedback gives you.

Here is an example of a situation in which feedback had been frozen for many years and how it was defrosted.

How to give feedback that gets results

You know when there is something you really need to tell someone but you hold back and decide not to tell them? You know when you have those imaginary conversations in your head with people that never translate into a real-life conversation? You know when you want to share feedback, but you are concerned about how someone will react? All of this builds up inside you, and the longer you leave it, the harder it is to give it. In our house we have a phrase we use when we are on the verge of losing our cool – yes, with three girls aged nine, nine and eleven, it happens! When we are close to losing control, we say, 'I'm going to go pop!' Usually this is enough of a warning for us to find a way to cool down before resolving whatever issue caused our blood to boil.

Giving feedback can feel like a high-pressure situation. Just like an over-inflated balloon, you might go POP or cause someone else to go POP because of the way you give them feedback or because of your timing.

A global head of marketing and global head of technology each told me the other despised them. These two executives were always disagreeing with one another. Their frequent disagreements were so rarely resolved that their teams actively tried to keep them apart. Hours were spent second-guessing decisions, attempting to avoid them having to meet, and interpreting emails rather than meeting face-to-face. The dysfunction became contagious; their respective teams started disagreeing with each other to the point where the CEO asked if I could help. This wasn't a recent development – it had been happening for several years. I told the CEO it was quite a miracle that they had achieved the results they had in spite of the complete breakdown in their relationship.

In my conversations with the two teams, I asked them to categorize their feedback into three areas: specifics about their processes, their organization, or where they thought it was personal. I call this the POP (Process, Organizational and Personal) process. Using this process, I tried to get them to articulate exactly what was broken between them. Some of it was history, some of it was misconception and some of it make-believe. The most important step in working through the issues in this relationship was getting really clear what was behind the original cause for conflict.

I created the POP Feedback Guide as a way to take the pressure out of any feedback opportunity by breaking down the real point of the feedback. Consider someone you want to give feedback to. Deconstruct exactly what the issue is and gather your thoughts using the POP Feedback Guide:

- **P – Process**
  Is this an issue with processes? Are the processes undocumented or unclear? Or are they in place but not being adhered to?
- **O – Organizational**
  Is this an organizational issue? Is there confusion or disagreement about who owns what?
- **P – Personal**
  Do you have examples of observed behavior that indicate an individual may not be interacting with you productively or professionally?

Once you have broken down which issues are Process, Organizational or Personal, don't go barreling in to start the conversation. Instead, follow these steps to improve the probability of a productive conversation:

1 **Time it precisely right.** Ask whether now is a good time or suggest a different time to talk.
2 **Share your intention.** Explain your reason for sharing the feedback so the recipient can understand what you want from the conversation.
3 **Don't sandwich it.** Despite common advice, do not start and end with a positive and put the difficult message in the middle. That technique distracts from your message and makes the positive comments seem insincere. Just get to the point.
4 **Offer to reciprocate.** Don't just *give* feedback; express your willingness to receive it too.
5 **Make it a habit.** This should not be a one-off event. If you do it regularly, this will become second nature for all of your key relationships.

Consider where you can use this approach yourself and how your team can apply it when they have feedback to give. You will solve many disagreements and eliminate a good deal of miscommunication and crossed wires.

If you don't tackle this proactively, your evil nemesis can quietly build and grow and just like the mythical Loch Ness Monster who lives in a desolate lake in Scotland, you may live in fear of who or what is lurking below the surface. It may knock your impact and influence off course if you don't tackle it head on.

Overcoming your evil nemesis

It is a common fallacy that a nemesis is one person. Your evil nemesis could be a group of people or a habit or set of behaviors you just can't shake. Like it or not, you probably have at least one (most of us do), and you may not know how to handle them. I frequently encounter people with an evil nemesis. Here are some recent examples:

- One executive has had her four biggest executive supporters leave the company simultaneously, and now the voice of one executive has the potential to cause her to quit or severely hamper her promotion prospects.
- Another executive has just joined a new company and the technical division is at odds with his creative team, causing endless spin cycles of distraction and confusion.
- An executive who decided to focus inwardly on his company and deliver incredible products for the last three years has now realized his network is dehydrated and out of date just at the very point when an acquisition means his executive role no longer exists.
- Another executive has been so swamped by delivering that he hasn't been able to focus his attention on upgrading and hiring the senior team needed to grow the business for the long term. His nose is barely above the waterline of activity and reactive projects.

Unlike in the movie *Beetlejuice* naming your nemesis three times won't make it appear or be resolved, but it will bring an awareness of something that you are likely to need to spend more time and attention on.

What or who is your evil nemesis?

Return to Chapter 1 and explore your Influence Bullseye and whether you have an evil nemesis that you need to face. Ask yourself whether your concern is based on observable behavior and evidence or stories you have made up in your head.

Who can help you tackle your evil nemesis? Do you have an issue to resolve, facts to clarify, relationships to build or something else? Can you use the POP framework to identify what the underlying causes may be?

While giving feedback is a much-discussed art, the act of receiving feedback is one that is not talked about enough.

We will next explore how to be a gracious receiver of feedback to further strengthen your trilingual expertise.

Stop being so defensive!

'Your response leaves me even more frustrated than the initial error!' That's the sort of thing you'll hear if you haven't developed the art of receiving feedback. How you respond to feedback can either escalate or de-escalate an issue. As I was writing this chapter, one of my clients emailed me a thread in which he was apoplectic about the response he got from one of his executive peers. 'Val,' he wrote, 'I am not being defensive, but look at his reply.' Here's a secret I have learned: Whenever anyone starts a sentence with 'I am not being defensive but...' there is a high probability that they are about to get defensive.

How you respond to feedback can either escalate or de-escalate an issue.

As I read the thread he forwarded, it was clear that he was in fact being defensive. He went into incredible detail about why the concerns that his peer had raised were not valid, explained why those concerns hadn't been caught by the CEO who had already approved it, and made factually incorrect statements. Most importantly, he had broken the three rules for receiving feedback:

1 **Pick up the phone.** Nothing contentious can be satisfactorily solved via email alone. First, take your emotional temperature. If you are furious, frustrated, annoyed, disappointed or ready to explode, step away from the keyboard and phone. Prepare what you want to say and then pick up the phone.
2 **Show appreciation for their feedback.** Say thank you to the person giving feedback for taking the time to do so, even if you don't like or agree with what they said.
3 **Stay curious.** Ask questions so you fully understand why they are giving you the feedback and how it translates across the creative, technical and business impact.

Most feedback fails because the recipient does not receive it, hear it, absorb it, reflect on it and *then* decide what action is needed as a result. If you fail to go through all of those steps when you receive feedback, the most dangerous thing starts to happen – people stop giving you feedback. How you give and respond to feedback can either make or break a relationship. I have worked with leaders who harbor grudges over seemingly minor issues, tainting productivity for years to come.

We have explored in detail the art of giving and receiving feedback as an individual. Next we will explore how your business seeks and creates an environment where feedback is encouraged, prompted and fully explored. And we will look at what happens if it is ignored.

The leadership insulation layer

How did over five hundred families allegedly buy their kids' way into prestigious colleges? The courts will figure out the semantics of donations versus outright bribes along with who knew what when, but I know why this was able to go on for so long: the leadership insulation layer.

It's the same with any of the recent corporate disasters, whether it is Volkswagen, Wells Fargo or the latest scandal to hit the news. How does an issue become so widespread and go on for so long? Because the leadership insulation layer prevents those who could flag the issue from raising it, or it is so effectively filtered that the original intent is lost before it reaches its intended recipient.

The one-million dollar mistake

I was running an executive workshop for the CMO of a multibillion-dollar global organization. As we were uncovering what was holding them back from growing even faster, someone explained about the unexpected million-dollar miss. The names have been withheld, but the learning remains the same. A new initiative was reported to be going quite successfully. Everything was on track and goals were going to be hit – until there was a million-dollar miss. The dollar amount wasn't the issue; the issue was the surprise. I asked the CMO and her executive team to answer the 'Three Essential Explanations':

1 Did you know that the project was not going to hit its goals before the P&L was published?
2 Did others know but didn't tell you?
3 What needed to be in place for them to get this message to you sooner?

The team used the 'Results Deconstruction' to understand just what happened not just on this project but on a series of successful ones, too. You too can use this tool as part of your team reflections.

The Results Deconstruction

- **Why do you ask?** Being reflective with your successes and misses is a key component of a Galvanized Team that drives remarkable results. You will benefit from:
  - Learning insights so you can repeat the right results, and make any necessary modifications.
  - Creating an open two-way communication where it is easier for your team to provide candid feedback when goals aren't met, or you need early warning signs when projects may be going off-track.
  - Understanding the true root cause of your results so you react to the cause not the symptoms.
  - Slowing down long enough to shine a spotlight on the positive results that you are creating – these are not just for when goals are missed!

- **Who do you ask?**
  - Identify all those who participated in the initiative or who were impacted by it.
  - Decide who is best positioned to give you a range of viewpoints.
- **How do you ask?**
  - A combination of:
    - Online anonymous survey (Google forms has a great simple survey tool; SurveyMonkey works well too);
    - Small focus groups;
    - One-on-one interviews.
  - Emphasize confidentiality if it is truly confidential (don't pretend!).
  - You may decide to use someone not close to the project, from a different team or function, or an external expert, to encourage open dialogue and give you extra capacity to get the conclusions versus doing the data-gathering yourself.
  - NOTE: It's acceptable to ask different groups in different ways.
- **What do you ask?**
  - No more than ten questions, ideally five, with a mix of qualitative and quantitative responses.
  - Rate the effectiveness of the changes on a scale of 1–10, with 10 being the highest:
    - Overall success of ABC Initiative;
    - Clarity on the goals of the change;
    - Design/Decision phase;
    - Communication/Implementation phase;
    - Transition phase.
  - Sample questions for you to edit and pick from:
    - What were the goals of the changes?
    - What has been the impact on business results, customers and employees?
    - What went well that you would replicate?

- What would you change if you did it again?
- What are your top five pieces of advice to leaders going through future changes?
- **What happens next?**
  - Share key themes, outliers and insights with senior leaders.
  - Decide what you will adopt, consider and ignore.
  - Loop back with a recap of #2 so those who contributed know they have been heard and you have taken action!

And finally, do not let anyone call this a postmortem. Unless you work in a medical facility this is unlikely to be about life and death. Simply use The Results Deconstruction!

CHAPTER 3 RAPID RECAP

- Understand and support your strong symbiotic relationships.
- Identify and seek to improve those symbiotic connections that need work.
- Assess yourself and your team with the trilingual executvie assessment.
- Ask 'so what?' for every initiative and understand the business impact on profit, revenue, market share and customers.
- Follow creative gurus to broaden your perspective.
- Ask for a metaphor when a technology peer explains a complex technical challenge.
- Reflect on how you can defrost feedback and increase the frequency and quality of the feedback that you receive.
- Deconstruct your results to replicate your successes.
- Create mechanisms and space to pause and reflect on mistakes and missteps.
- Consider where your insulation layers against feedback are holding you back.

CHAPTER FOUR

Building an innovative company

In order to build a rapid growth strategy you have to understand the elements of your company today that will propel you faster and those that will inhibit your speed. In this chapter you will learn how to dispel common innovation myths and take an inventory of your company's likelihood of creating innovation. You will also discover how to rapidly create a strategy and organization that will set you on the path to exponential growth.

CHAPTER TOPICS

- Simple myths of innovation dispelled
- The Innovation Inventory Measurement Tool
- Your leapfrog strategy and organization
- Your CEO succession
- Mixing in the right pipelines of talent

Simple myths of innovation dispelled

Everyone wants to know the secret to creating continuous innovation that fuels rapid growth. Innovation is so critical to success
that it's easy to fall prey to the myths surrounding it. Is innovation rooted in pure luck? Why are some companies more
innovative than others? How did Blackberry go from over 50
per cent market share in 2009 to less than 3 per cent today?

Before we explore what it takes to build an innovative organization, there are a number of myths that need to be examined,
debunked and thrown out for their level of ridiculousness. Don't
let these four common myths distract you from creating the new
product experience that your customers need.

Myth 1: Innovative products will motivate your employees

Reality: It isn't enough to work for an innovative company with
incredible products; you need to pay attention and find innovative
approaches to making your employees delighted. For example, the
number one complaint from any employee who has to work with
customers is the customers! Listen to anyone working in the
customer service industry, from airlines to hotels, and they will
share horror stories about rude, obnoxious or unreasonable customers. Uber may be criticized for how they disrupt new markets and
for some of their questionable executive decisions, but when they
first launched, they decided to turn the customer relationship upside
down and experiment with incentivizing customers to be consider-
ate and polite to their employees by getting drivers to rate customers
after each trip. The secret customer rating (which you could find out
if you asked your Uber driver nicely) gave you a ranking of one to
five stars depending on your punctuality and behavior during your
trip. Higher-scoring customers get picked up faster and eventually
may earn an invitation to the exclusive Uber VIP club, a premium
service that matches the highest-ranking customers with the top-
performing drivers, for faster, higher-quality service. This soon
became so much of a worst-kept secret, Uber changed it so your

rating was visible, which still had the intended consequence of people concerned about their rating, bringing a different perspective on customer service. Ask yourself whether you know the greatest annoyances for your employees and how you could fix them.

Myth 2: Only proven success defines an innovative leader

Reality: Multiple failures do not disqualify a leader from being known as innovative, quite the opposite. Ask any founder of a start-up; they will share multiple unsuccessful business ideas and ventures, yet they still attract investors and further rounds of funding. Often you cannot pave the road to success until you have hit a few dead ends. Many believe the key is to avoid mistakes; it's not. The key is to avoid the blame game, to be rapidly curious, and to consider and commit to making changes as a leader when projects fail. Are you creating an environment in your business that punishes failure and shames people or one that uses failure as a launching pad? In Chapter 10 we further explore this when we look at Rapid Growth Done Wrong and how getting fired or pushed out can be the best thing that has ever happened to you.

Myth 3: You need to go offsite to innovate

Reality: While retreats, away-days and think tanks may create occasional breakthrough thinking, innovation needs to be an everyday affair. If you don't build innovation into your company's daily life and expectations, it won't happen. Don't rely on a crutch for your creativity. Amazon's key principle of 'invent and simplify' is at the heart of their success in creating rapid, endless innovation. In my corporate career as part of Amazon Fashion's leadership team, we asked for examples of innovative ideas at interview, assessed employees against it during performance reviews, and only promoted leaders who had proven success in building an

If you don't build innovation into your company's daily life and expectations, it won't happen.

75

innovative team. Can you confidently say that you are building innovation into every aspect of your business?

Myth 4: Everyone needs the same zip code

Reality: It's true that Yahoo revised their telecommuting policies and nixed working from home, claiming that having everyone in the same office is in the best interests of team cohesion and rapid growth, but it is a fallacy that proximity drives innovation. When Xbox was innovating and creating the Kinect camera, we had developers in Israel, creative studios in England, hardware teams in Washington and a smattering of teams in between. In a world where finding and keeping the best talent gets tougher, forcing people into the same zip code is not only short-sighted, it stifles the unique ideas, perspectives and energy that different people bring.

The Innovation Inventory Measurement Tool

Now that we have dispelled the common innovation myths, we can explore the innovation spiral that successful companies accelerate through. Build and develop each of the nine innovation catapult points, shown in Figure 4.1, to accelerate up the spiral. If you lose focus on these areas, it will propel you backwards into oblivion. To comprehensively evaluate where you are today, assess your organization with the Innovation Inventory Measurement Tool below, scoring one point for each statement you can agree with.

Read the following 24 statements and see how many you can say a wholehearted 'yes' to:

1 We create freedom to play and experiment.
2 Innovation is linked to our long-term business goals.
3 If there is a good idea, we rapidly fund it with people and dollars.

4 We are quick to sunset failing projects gracefully.

5 We recognize speed is sometimes more important than perfection.

6 New ideas flow between functions, locations and seniority.

7 Most of our energy is spent on customers, products and profits, not internal politics.

8 We incorporate the voice of youth in our product strategy and community outreach.

9 We encourage meeting-free days and we create freedom and space to think.

10 We don't care where you work or how you work as long as you deliver your results and act according to the company values.

11 Our pivotal leaders have strong personal followings.

12 We take time to learn from successes and failures without blame.

13 We are candid and transparent in our communication to customers and employees.

14 Our employee and industry communication is inspiring and innovative.

FIGURE 4.1 Innovation Inventory Measurement Tool

15 It is OK to challenge our status quo, regardless of hierarchy.

16 Our communication to our customers raises eyebrows, grabs attention and makes an impact.

17 We regularly listen to our top people and hear personal stories of how they would like the workplace to improve, and then we take action.

18 We assess for innovation ability and appetite when we hire.

19 We have alternative approaches to acquiring expertise and talent.

20 We have a robust personal referral program that delivers high-quality candidate referrals.

21 We personally develop our employees in creative and unique ways.

22 Our egos do not prevent us from seeking expert help; even the most successful leaders seek ways to further accelerate their success.

23 We reward behaviors and attempts at innovation, not just success.

24 We reward against company, team and individual achievements in that order.

Your Innovation Inventory Measurement score:

Here is how to interpret your results:

- **19–24 Congratulations!** You lead the way in creating a culture that accelerates innovation; do not lose sight of the high standards you have set as you grow. Create your leapfrog strategy and organization then identify areas you need to focus on for your future growth.
- **13–18 Nearly there!** You stand out from the crowd as a company that innovates. You have a few blind spots; focus on those quickly and you will create outstanding results.
- **7–12 Danger Zone!** You have some great practices, but you have a number of gaps that will cripple your ability to build great products and delight customers. Pay attention to what you are missing and develop a plan to accelerate changes in those areas.

- <6 **Blackberry Inc.** Watch out: your competition will shortly pass you by. If you are not losing customers now, you soon will be. To drive business growth, you need to radically overhaul how you run your company. Get help. Fast.

This assessment is only as useful as the concrete action you take as a result. You may be asking yourself why this is important, or what you need to do next. Good! That is explained in Chapters 5–8, but if you are impatient, here are five fast actions you can take tomorrow:

1 *Take a seat.* Lack of connection hinders innovation and creativity. Go and sit with your teams and experience their work environment. Listen to them and observe how they spend their day. Ask them in the moment what changes would improve how fast they get results.
2 *Look in the mirror.* To inspire and motivate others, you have to love your job and be having fun. You can see this when you watch and listen to leaders describe their job and their company. Are you in your 'perfect ten' job? Do your eyes sparkle when you talk about your company and your role there?
3 *The contrarian lunch.* Gather five of your most contrarian employees and invite them to a discussion about your current vision and strategy. Ask them what is holding it back, how you can accelerate innovation, and what you personally can do as a leader to improve the probability of success.
4 *The best and the worst.* Take the team from your most innovative product and the last product that failed. Have a conversation with both teams together about what worked and why it worked, and what failed and why it failed. What patterns and trends can you see? When Tara Moeller was interm general manager of CamelBak, she ran a '*best of the worst review*' with her leadership team to highlight what was learned from the projects that failed to get off the ground.

5 *Your customers' shoes.* Starbucks requires every manager to work as a barista for a week. They can't start at corporate HQ until they have earned their 'Green Apron' at a retail store. Of course, they learn more than just how to make the perfect cappuccino, they learn about the company from the front line where customers matter. How can you get your leaders to go back to the floor today?

Your leapfrog strategy and organization

Now that you have gained insight into your own company and how innovative you are, it's time to catapult innovation by looking ahead to create your leapfrog strategy and organization (see Figure 4.2). Too many leaders hire for their current company rather than for the size and scale it will be in five years' time. I explore this in detail in my first book, *Thoughtfully Ruthless: The Key to Exponential Growth*. By assessing the capability and capacity of your organization against your future business, you begin to understand the gap you need to close to execute on your strategy, build your leapfrog organization and catapult to success.

Too many leaders hire for their current company rather than for the size and scale it will be in five years' time.

Since rapid growth is the new norm, you need to build your organization of the future, today. Doing so means you will likely go through the Intentional Annoyance Phase and displease many of your existing people in order to realize the growth your company is capable of – but that is necessary if you truly want to catapult innovation.

The reality is that 75 per cent of hiring slows you down rather than speeds you up because of the catastrophic fault most hiring managers make: they hire for their immediate needs today, not for what they need in the future. You need to be ruthless, in a thoughtful way, with your resources. You have to approach your hiring, growth and approach to change in a completely different way. By adhering to the following steps, you can create your own leapfrog strategy.

Step 1: Pick a time horizon

It starts first with knowing the size and scale of your business in two years' time – but don't get stuck on the time horizon. When I used to work at Land Rover, our strategy sessions focused on ten years out, so we would start with a five-year leap. When I work with rapidly growing consumer electronics companies, we focus on a two-year leap. Pick a time horizon to coincide with your next significant growth leap.

Step 2: Know your current and future business

First take a look at your business today and note your profit, revenue and employees. Consider what current markets you are in, which industries and what products and services you offer. Now leap ahead to your first leap. What will be different? Ask yourself these questions:

- What new markets will we be in?
- What new products will we offer?
- What new services might we develop?
- What new distribution channels should we consider?
- Who will our new customer be?
- Where will our locations be based?
- How will we have grown (by acquisition, organically)?

Step 3: Live in your future world

Next, imagine you are living in your business in your two-year leap. Start by considering your own role and that of your CEO: how will that be different? What skills and capabilities will you need? Which of those do you have already? Now ask yourself the toughest question every CEO has to ask themselves: is it time for me to fire myself? If you are not the CEO, and you are a member of the board or the executive team, this may be a more difficult conversation to have. But if you avoid it, you are suffocating the growth and innovation possibilities of your company, so you have a choice to make.

It may not be as radical as firing yourself or your CEO, but it may be time to decide that you do not have the perfect CEO for your leapfrog organization, which we explore later in this chapter. But assuming you have the right CEO now, take a look at your executive team and ask yourself these questions:

- What are the pivotal capabilities we need to support our future growth?
- Which of those do we have today in our existing executive team?
- Which can we develop and grow?
- What do we need to acquire?

Now for each executive assess the following:

- Can he or she rapidly grow in place?
- Does he or she need support to stretch and grow?
- Is he or she mismatched (a blocker or unlikely to scale)?

Step 4: Develop a plan to leapfrog to your future world

To develop a plan to leapfrog into your future world, you need to address the various situations you find yourself in with your executives.

GROW-IN-PLACE EXECUTIVES

Take these executives that can rapidly grow in place and share with them the expectations of how you see the role and company growing, what you need from them and how they can accelerate their impact. These are the leaders that many CEOs spend the least time with, when, in fact, they should be spending the most. The return on effort of spending your energy and time with these executives is astronomical.

NEEDS-SUPPORT EXECUTIVES

Be clear on what support these executives need. Is it context, skill building, technical ability or personal development? Create simple, clear development goals and communicate them concisely. Dr Seligman's research on positive psychology proves that focusing on someone's strengths is far more productive than trying to fix their weaknesses, so don't waste your energy. What do they need on their team to complement their strengths? What support can you give them in mentoring or is there a coach who can help them specifically make progress against their goals?

MISMATCHED EXECUTIVES

I have never met an executive who has regretted acting too fast. Too often a leader will say to me, if only I had acted six months ago, I would have saved all of that time, prevented others from quitting, and gotten better business results. You know who these people are. Ask yourself if they are critical to long- or short-term projects and how you can redesign their job so it plays to their strengths. If that isn't possible, create an exit plan for them.

Step 5: Redefine today's roles for tomorrow

Finally, scope your roles on your executive team so they are targeted for the size and scale of your future company. If you have a VP of sales and your current revenues are $2 billion and you will grow to $6 billion in two years, hire someone who has experience managing an organization with $6–10 billion in sales. That is the fastest way to catapult your growth. Do this for every role. In parallel, you can also help teach the current VP how to scale by having them surround themselves with more senior executives that they can learn from inside and outside of the organization.

FIGURE 4.2 The leapfrog strategy

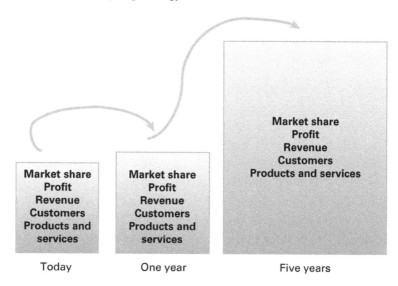

| Today | One year | Five years |

From strategy to execution at Xbox

When Don Mattrick was appointed as CEO of Xbox in 2007, Xbox was fast becoming the runt of the Microsoft litter. While teenage boys in North America loved Xbox, it was a problem for Microsoft. It culminated in a $1 billion write-off because of the 'red-ring-of-death' quality problems, and the fact that Nintendo's Wii had become the must-have toy of the moment. We were in danger of becoming irrelevant unless we broke away from our strict focus on North American males aged 16 to 22 who liked shooting and racing games.

I was running the leadership and organization development for the Xbox division, and in Don's first week I shared some of my views on the leadership team and the changes that needed to happen for us to turn the business around. He said, 'Let's spend a day on this next week.' I went to his home in Vancouver, Canada, and we talked for a day about how the business would grow in the next three years and what the implications would be for the leadership and organization. We created a plan for what we would change when. That became the basis for the three-year plan for the Xbox business.

It would be easy to stop here – many CEOs and executives do. They talk about the theory that the VP of Operations needs more global experience, but they don't act on it. They know that the president of the European office is in the biggest job of his life and unlikely to succeed without additional support, but they fail to give direct, specific feedback and provide specialist help to learn new skills or change behavior. Don't be like them. Now that you have identified the gaps in your leapfrog organization, develop a plan to get you where you want to go. This has to be the number one priority of your CEO and board if you truly want to build an innovative company.

Every day you spend with a mismatched executive in a role, or settling for the people you have in place, is a day you could have spent hiring a replacement or benefiting from someone with a grander vision, greater insights or a higher capacity for growth. A leapfrog organization is a perpetual machine. Once you create one at the top of your organization, it cascades throughout your business with ease. If you address this at the top, it will bring up the question that is unfortunately whispered in hallways more than it is talked about in boardrooms: who will be our next CEO?

Your CEO succession

When the boards of Twitter and Square decided to share Jack Dorsey as CEO, it was not part of a clever strategic move. Twitter's CEO role was vacant for nine months while the board performed a CEO search. Only 31 per cent of companies report having a robust CEO succession plan; this means that board-rooms and investors are largely ignoring one of the greatest barriers to maintaining and accelerating innovation.

The greatest mistake boards and CEOs make with succession planning is leaving it as the responsibility of human resources. It is a standing joke in many Fortune 500 companies that HR teams decide to change either the succession planning or the performance review process every few years to give HR something to do. While this joke is grounded in far more reality than anyone would like to admit, the greatest problem with succession planning is that it is not fully owned by boards or the executive team, and it becomes a tick-box exercise rather than a meaningful conversation.

When Steve Ballmer was still CEO of Microsoft, he instituted annual succession-planning discussions as part of an annual 'people review' process that every divisional president took part in. Although he was mimicking Jack Welch's GE people review process, the idea got a bit lost in translation – because instead of vibrant, challenging conversations about top talent, weeks and weeks were spent on perfecting and scripting PowerPoint presentations rather than having honest dialogues. Ironically, despite all of the man-hours spent on Steve's people review process, when Steve himself resigned as CEO, it took nine months to backfill his role with Satya Nadella.

To truly create an innovative organization you don't need succession planning, you need succession action.

Many succession-planning efforts are futile because they focus too deeply in an organization. Microsoft isn't the only place where I have seen weeks of effort wasted in fake conversations about middle managers when everyone knows that there is a vacuum at the top of the organization that nobody wants to talk about or acknowledge. To truly create an innovative organization you don't need succession planning, you need succession action. This is why I use the Succession Action Program (SAP), which goes beyond planning and into real action. (See Figure 4.3.)

CEO Succession Action Program

Listed on the Canadian Stock exchange with 12 per cent year-over-year growth, Wanted Analytics had developed a strong,

FIGURE 4.3 Succession Action Program

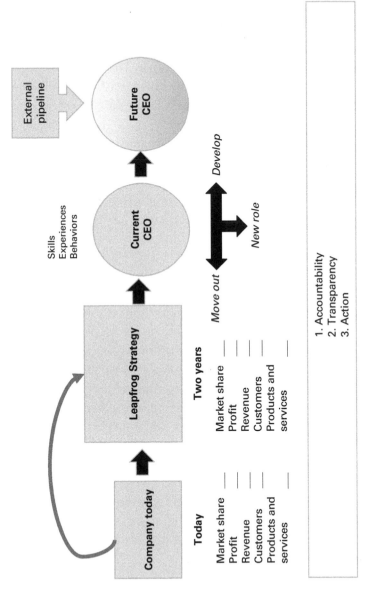

External
pipeline

Skills
Experiences
Behaviors

Future
CEO

Current
CEO

Develop

New role

Move out

Leapfrog Strategy

Two years

Market share ___
Profit ___
Revenue ___
Customers ___
Products and ___
services

Company today

Today

Market share ___
Profit ___
Revenue ___
Customers ___
Products and ___
services

1. Accountability
2. Transparency
3. Action

steady business providing big data analytics to Fortune 500 companies. But Tim Baskerville, chairman of the board, knew the growth should be sharper and the progress more rapid. When he looked to the leapfrog company of the future, he knew it could grow at a significantly higher rate. The existing CEO had done a stellar job until now, but as Tim and the board looked two years out and assessed the current CEO, they knew what they had to do. It was time for a new CEO, and they made that search their number one priority.

Like many small companies, Wanted Analytics did not have any internal candidates waiting to take over the top spot, but there was a perfect candidate sitting on Wanted's board: Meredith Amdur, an investor who had served on the board for the previous two years. She was currently head of strategy for DirectTV and her background at Deloitte and Microsoft made her a perfect candidate. Tim and the board followed the three factors critical to the success of the Succession Action Program: first they took full accountability and made it their immediate number one priority; second, they were transparent; and third, they took decisive action.

The new CEO became my client and I supported her transition as CEO. There was an immediate mechanism for knowing this was a successful decision. In Amdur's first three months the stock price rose 37 per cent; no earnings were reported during that time, so the growth in value was entirely from the investors' confidence in the new strategic direction from the CEO. Twelve months later Amdur led the sale of the company to CEB at a remarkable premium price. Amdur was able to invigorate the sales channel and find innovative ways to serve existing and new customers while intentionally retaining the full executive team during what could have been a tumultuous transition from the previous CEO of eight years.

Some boards may well have still been sitting around a table deliberating whether it was the right decision to replace the CEO, trying to decide whether the timing was right or whether to give the current incumbent some feedback and hope they could make the leap in performance expectations. In just over a year, the Wanted Analytics board was able to realize the true value of their investment and get a new partner to accelerate their growth.

Wanted was able to tap their board for potential CEO candidates, which is one of many pivotal sources for candidates for your Succession Action Program. I often find that leaders deep within an organization are better equipped to line up potential talent to join their team than the executives in the board room who should in theory find it easier to make connections and find introductions.

Either way, it is time to stop succession planning and move on to succession action.

Mixing in the right pipelines of talent

A European IT consulting firm, Sema Group, bought a medical services company from the British government with the intent of innovating its services and turning it into a profit machine. I was part of the leadership team that had to make the promises from the acquisition a reality. Except we made one ginormous mistake: we failed to realize the extent to which there was a void of certain groups of talent during the due diligence phase, and we neglected to rapidly develop a plan to address it. This was a prime example of rapid growth done wrong. We grew our top-line revenue numbers but created a huge strategic distraction.

Doctors, nurses and administrators in benefits offices around the UK had an essential role in assessing whether those claiming disability benefit were fit to return to work. The government decided to outsource this service in 1999, and Sema Group (which became part of Schlumberger Sema in a subsequent merger) won the contract. Sema had a vision: they wanted to provide occupational health services to corporations, so they viewed the government project as a foundation for credibility as a health service provider. But due diligence failed to surface the most critical risk to the investment: a substantial lack of business talent and lack of awareness and understanding of the business of occupational health.

Sema was a for-profit consulting firm. Its clients included government organizations, and they had previously won contracts from former government organizations. Sema acquired the IT team and the customer support team, but the company had never employed medical experts before. What soon became painfully clear was the chasm that existed between the medical experts and the business experts. This became the greatest conflict, and the ensuing confusion distracted from attaining what the acquisition had hoped to achieve. Transition from a government service to a for-profit business was a greater transition than originally expected. We could have speeded it up if we had better managed the multiple pipelines of talent.

In the heat of the moment it isn't easy to step back and see what is happening, especially in the post-acquisition flurry of change and activity. Add to that a UK parliamentary select committee investigation into the service and the government's decision to outsource, which made for an intense year of lawsuits, employment tribunals and painful conflict.

Just like baking cupcakes, you need exactly the right ingredients to build an innovative organization.

Just like baking cupcakes, you need exactly the right ingredients to build an innovative organization. If your measurements are slightly off, you won't get the perfect results. Unfortunately, too many companies neglect certain groups of talent, ignoring them like the ingredients hidden at the back of the kitchen cupboard. It isn't until you decide you need them and mix them into your recipe that you realize the results are quite rancid!

When we acquired the medical services group, we neglected the medical staff, failing to seek to understand, engage, involve and develop them. Yet they were so critical to our success. Which pockets of talent are you neglecting in your organization?

To avoid making the same mistakes, you can follow the Five Innovation Talent Steps (FITS) to make sure that your organization FITS together all of the important elements to accelerate innovation.

Five Innovation Talent Steps (FITS)

1 **Leadership capability.** You have strong leaders in addition to individual contributors and subject-matter experts.
2 **Abundance of future talent.** Your pipeline of rising stars and potential future experts and leaders is strong.
3 **Enviable professional development.** You value and invest in developing professional capabilities.
4 **Inspiring communication.** You create inspiring and energizing communication that is unique and evokes action.
5 **External credibility.** Your reputation precedes you for innovation in your field and function.

Once you are confident that you have five strong steps, take a look across the five steps for each of your talent groups (marketing, developers, sales, creative, IT, business development and so forth). What patterns emerge? What steps can you immediately take to address the gaps?

You now have a detailed picture of where you want your company to be in two years' time, and how likely your current team and organization are to get you there. With this insight you can create a plan to rapidly accelerate that journey. Meanwhile, you have a company to inspire, and Chapter 5 explores just how you do that.

CHAPTER 4 RAPID RECAP

1 Evaluate your company using the Innovation Inventory Measurement Tool.

2 Identify and dispel your own company myths behind your rapid growth.

3 Go and walk in the shoes of your customer to truly understand your business.

4 Gather your employees who offer contrarian views to your own and really listen to them.

5 Get on the front line of your business: answer calls, serve customers and understand the reality of your products and services.

6 Ask how your current products, services, distribution channels, customers and locations will change in three years.

7 Time-travel ahead and build the talent you need in the future today.

8 Create your Succession Action Plan around you.

9 Hire people who have managed businesses of the size and scale of your future projections.

10 Rapid growth done wrong occurs when you blindly chase revenue and market share without considering the strategic barriers to execution.

CHAPTER FIVE

How to influence and communicate with anyone

This chapter demonstrates that despite the radical innovations in technology, services and media that have occurred in the last 25 years, many leaders are still leading like it is 1992. We had grandiose claims that there would be a paperless office a decade ago, yet paper is still far from being eliminated. We add new communication technologies into workplaces in the name of efficiency, but often they simply add complexity and distraction. Despite all of the modern technology available for communication, including Slack, Facebook, Twitter and Microsoft Teams, habits across companies have not changed: the number one business communication is still email. Yet employees have input overload with work communication, social media channels, watches, glasses and even their umbrellas and speakers buzzing or talking to them, sharing information, and ultimately distracting their attention.

Therefore to create success, to get your next round of funding or that strategic partnership, or to work across internal functions successfully, you have to adopt new ways of influencing by communicating based on the realities of today. This chapter provides a collection of tools, examples and interviews with leaders who share influencing techniques that have worked for them and the results that followed. We will tap into your creative side and learn from many musicians and artists about how to replace your current habits with new ones and experiment with new ways of influencing and communicating.

CHAPTER TOPICS
- How to capture attention and deliver messages like Banksy
- The communication sieve
- Why music can fuel your creative communications
- Accelerating effective communication
- Ask better questions

How to capture attention and deliver messages like Banksy

Banksy is a British street artist whose identity is a mystery, yet how he engages with his audience provides us with insights that will help you communicate with anyone. Compare how Banksy does it with how you communicate in a typical day or week at work.

Create a provocative PR stunt

Banksy gets attention in unique ways: once he set up a seemingly innocent artist's stall on the banks in Venice and painted a humungous picture of a cruise ship crammed into a tiny waterway in protest of the cruise ships overtaking Venice and their environmental impact on the city. He eventually got kicked out as he didn't have the proper permits, but he was really protesting because he had never been invited to the prestigious Venice Biennale Art Festival. This stunt earned him more attention, media focus and critical acclaim than attending the festival itself.

Make the most of eight seconds

Museum attendees only spend an average of eight seconds looking at each piece of art, according to a British study at the Tate Gallery, but Banksy has managed to find new ways to get his audience to pay attention to his work. He created a treasure hunt in New York; not only did you have to find the art installation across the city of New York, you had to call a number to hear him describing in detail what he created and why. One installation was a truck filled with stuffed animal puppets with their heads poking out of cracks in the back squeaking for help. I called the number on the back and it said:

> This is a piece of sculpture art, and I know what you're thinking, 'Isn't it a bit subtle?' This truck contains over 60 cuddly soft toys on the road to a swift death. However, in order to bring them to life, four professional puppeteers are required, strapped into bucket seats, dressed entirely in black lycra, pulling on an array of levers with each limb and given only one toilet break a day – proving that the only sentient beings held in lower esteem than livestock are mime artists.

Banksy certainly got my attention for more than eight seconds on that one!

Are you provoking and inspiring your employees and encouraging interaction? Many leaders unfortunately revert to email. When I work with executives and observe communication between leaders and employees, I notice that it is tedious, monotonous and primarily email focused – and three-quarters of it never actually gets read!

Don't follow the crowd and get lost in the hype

Banksy sold his artworks for $60 each at a discreet stall next to New York's Central Park in 2014. There was no PR or hype, and he only made $420 in sales when each piece was worth over $200,000. Imagine the surprise when these lucky customers got their art home, assuming they saw the news or someone told them they had bought a genuine Banksy for a fraction of the value! Many leaders follow the crowd and the latest trends and hype, from which company to work at to which latest management catchphrases or buzzwords to use – without fully understanding them. If you pay attention to what you love and create your own following among your employees, you will create your own masterpiece rather than miss out on it like many New Yorkers that day.

Don't take yourself seriously

My mentor Alan Weiss always tells me that self-effacing humor is the best, most effective and safest kind of humor! Banksy continually ridicules himself and the world of art, including those bidding on his art at Sotheby's. Just after one of his pieces sold for $866,000 at a London auction house, an automatic shredder set off and the piece disappeared and started to disintegrate into hundreds of pieces before stopping halfway. You can see a link to the video on www. rapidgrowthdoneright.com. Leaders who can laugh at themselves create an atmosphere where it is acceptable to be less than perfect. If you can be transparent and authentic and laugh along the way, it takes the pressure off

Just after one of his pieces sold for $866,000 at a London auction house, an automatic shredder set off

and increases the likelihood that your teams will have fun. In an interview with the UK's *Independent* newspaper Banksy shared how the piece of art was meant to be completely destroyed, but the mechanism jammed.[1] The piece, originally called *The Girl with a*

Balloon, was renamed *Love is in the Bin*. Again, another great example of making the most of things when something goes wrong.

Tap into your heritage to get your message across

One of my vague claims to fame is that the elusive Banksy and I shared a childhood hangout in England: the Tropicana in the seaside resort of Weston-super-Mare, which several decades ago was a fun outdoor swimming pool with giant plastic pineapple slides, wave machines and a fake ice rink made from wax. The pool has been abandoned for a decade while landowners and council members have argued what to do with it, so who better to breathe life into the graveyard than the secretive Banksy? Innovation occurs when you are outside your comfort zone. Different ideas are born in such places. Banksy transformed the decrepit pool into an art collection from 50 global artists; it featured dead princesses, ducks covered in oil, terrible prizes of fish fingers in plastic bags, and whales trying to escape captivity. The Dismaland Bemusement called itself 'The most disappointing new visitor attraction' on its website at the time, but in true Banksy style, his online memorials of his art and message are often only fleeting. You can still see a small selection of the exhibition photos at www.dismaland.co.uk.

Don't let others' opinion dent your self-worth

Creative geniuses like Banksy have to continue against all the odds, regardless of what others think. That requires a strong sense of self-worth, where you don't worry about what others think or how they will react. As I work with successful creative leaders to accelerate growth and innovation, I have noticed that this characteristic is what delineates the remarkable from the good. Banksy is an exceptional role model here. Press and visitor reaction is irrelevant to him. Banksy told *Juxtapoz* in an exclusive secret email interview, 'My satisfaction level is independent of your opinion. If I feel a piece has worked, there's nothing you can say that will take that away. And the flip side is, if I know it's failed, there's nothing you can say that would make it okay.' Do you have Banksy's level of personal peace?

Be open to the unexpected

When creating a piece with a crashed Cinderella carriage, Banksy saw the carriage surrounded by a ring of paparazzi, and the flash bulbs created an effect making the pumpkin look like it was being lit by flickering candles. In his *Juxtapoz* interview, Banksy said it was a complete surprise, but he loved the results. You can see the video at www.rapidgrowthdoneright.com. This scene reminds me of the tragic death of Princess Diana in 1997. Every piece of art will trigger different emotions, thoughts and actions. Are you and your team constantly open to embracing the unexpected? How can you use art to share your key messages or inspiration with your team?

Allow frugality to fuel you

Banksy tells *Juxtapoz* that his miniscule budget created one of the most original pieces at the Dismaland exhibition. He couldn't spend $8,000 a week on an exclusive Jenny Holzer electronic sign, so he asked Jenny to record her slogans audibly so he could play them over the public address system, free of charge. 'She liked the idea and said she'd never done anything like it in 40 years. So now we have a totally original Jenny Holzer.' I have seen leaders challenge their teams to solve a problem with limited or no budget to provoke and inspire a flood of new creative ideas, and it's worked.

Hold your events at Banksy-inspired locations

The most remarkable locations where I have run events for teams to spark creativity are a stark room in a Seattle library overlooking the city skyline, a luxury car showroom surrounded by vintage Bentleys and Ferraris in Santa Barbara, and a cabin in the middle of the woods surrounded by snow and frozen waterfalls.

Even if you missed Banksy's five-week-only exhibition in the seaside resort of Weston-super-Mare, England, you can still view his exhibition online via www.rapidgrowthdoneright.com, where you will find a discussion guide that you can use to talk to your team about what Banksy can teach you about creativity.

Little and often works

Banksy creates powerful, frequent messages, which beats long, rambling stories. Can you do the same? Banksy has gone beyond what we expect of him – from one-off installations to curating a thought-provoking exhibition that raises questions about immigration, corruption, injustice and animal cruelty with elite artists from around the globe. How are you and your team pushing the limits of what is expected of you? Where can you take your team to provoke their thinking?

Not everyone's brain works like yours

Banksy appeals to a variety of ways to consume information: visual, auditory and short, sharp bursts of provocative statements. Our brains are all wired differently – yet we communicate en masse, and we are prone to talk AT people not with people. If you lead 5, 50, 500, or 5000 people, chances are you use the one-to-many approach – everyone gets the email / all hands / whitepaper. But if you were really accommodating the different ways in which people consume information, you would provide the SAME information in multiple ways. This may sound like a painful waste of time, but it is really an opportunity to make sure you are communicating with everyone.

The communication sieve

What percentage of your intentions are getting achieved with your communications? Let's take an email message through the

FIGURE 5.1 The communication sieve

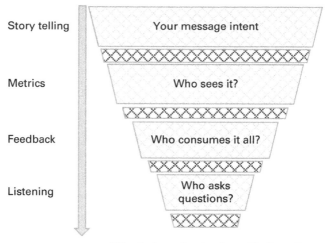

Who truly understands and believes?

communication sieve (Figure 5.1). Ask yourself how many of your emails are opened? Now consider of those who open your email: how many read all the way to the end? Of those that read to the end, how many questions do you get back to test their understanding? Those questions (if you even get them) help you see where they fully understood or where they need more clarity. Then, finally, you have to ask whether your recipients truly understood and really believe what you shared with them. Now that is a lot of questions and ifs and buts, yet that is the reality of how we receive, absorb and respond to information. If we now layer on the complexity of a neurodiverse brain, we have more to consider.

I knew who Peter Shankman was because I have benefited from one of the companies he founded, Help A Reporter Out. What I only recently discovered was that he is an expert in neurodiversity and hosts the number one podcast on Attention Deficit and Hyperactivity Disorder (ADHD). In his book, *Faster Than Normal*, he offers advice for those who want to live happily with someone with ADHD. For *Rapid Growth, Done*

Right, I specifically asked Peter for his most important advice for those with an ADHD brain. He shared his top three:

1 Stop caring what other people think. Do what works for you. You're different. Embrace that and act like it.
2 Eliminate choice. Two choices are better than ten.
3 Exercise, get enough sleep and eat healthily, all of which allow you to use your ADHD faster brain to its best ability. Self-care has to come first.

Based on my own research and studying, I now consider myself a student of neurodiversity as I recently discovered that I, too, have the gift of an ADHD brain.

We've discovered how art and our brain make-up impact how we communicate and influence others, so let us look at how we can embrace music to unleash our creativity.

Why music can fuel your creative communications

Listening to music changes your mood both positively and negatively, depending on whether you like the music. It can help you focus, relax and get your message across, no matter who your audience is. Think about it: If you could watch the same scene in a movie and change the background music from upbeat to slow and dramatic, you would experience entirely different emotions.

Listening to music changes your mood both positively and negatively.

iHeartMedia's Vice President of Business Development Jodi Dewey notes just how important music is in how you remember. She shared this with me in an interview: *'Think about how music plays a role in your memories... I can pick a song that takes me back to every significant moment.'* It is true in your personal life, so how can you leverage this in your work life?

Australia's *CEO Magazine* asked all of their top CEOs what song they played before an important board meeting and compiled a playlist for all of their conference attendees; it ranged from Frank Sinatra's 'New York New York' to Avicii's 'The Nights'. When Steve Ballmer was CEO of Microsoft, he used to pick a theme tune to run out to during the company meeting. The most memorable for me was Survivor's 'Eye of the Tiger', during a particularly rough few years of poor market share growth.

We can learn valuable lessons from musicians of all stripes, even DJs like David Guetta. Now you may not expect to learn lessons from a DJ who is more at home in clubs in Ibiza and New York than sharing leadership and innovation lessons, but there are surprising insights to gain. Here are eight lessons from David Guetta that you can incorporate into your communications:

- **Anticipation brings more happiness than the event itself:** I might be getting past this as I age, but it has been proven that anticipation of an event brings more happiness than the event itself. When I last saw David Guetta at Encore Beach Club in Las Vegas, he certainly made sure this was true as we waited for five hours for his set to start. Recently ranked eighth on *Forbes*'s list of highest-paid DJs, he put on a remarkable performance, and the crowd was captivated.[2]
- **Remember the triple-three rule:** Prepare the beginning and the end well. The first three and the last three minutes are the most important parts of any speech. In between, pick three points you want your audience to remember and plan your talk around that.
- **Location, location, location, location:** A sunny beach pool in Las Vegas made a delightful venue. Influencing the venue where you speak to your team really matters. You might not always get to choose sunshine, but crowded rooms, bland backdrops and windowless venues will not inspire your audience and they won't listen to you.
- **Get your audience involved:** During one part of Guetta's set, he mutes the speakers to get the crowd to sing along. The tune

says, 'Work hard,' then he mutes it as the audience sings the next line, 'Play hard.' This repeats several times much to the crowd's enjoyment. I have watched far too many leaders talk at their audience as though they were speaking to cardboard cutouts, not real live people who are waiting to get involved. Now I don't suggest a Guetta-like chant, but do interact with your audience and involve them.

- **Go in with a bang:** Leaders often struggle with the start of their talks. Guetta led with his music. He didn't start by getting on the mic and saying, 'Hello, it is great to be here. I hope the traffic wasn't too terrible. Isn't the weather fabulous?' Cut the inane ramblings when you first appear in front of your audience and start with a bang.
- **Leave them wanting more:** Guetta didn't play 30 seconds of every tune he has ever written, clumsily rushing and mixing in everything and saying, 'If only I had more time.' He picked his set, stuck with the plan and left people wanting to hear more. Most leaders cram in too much information when talking, which causes them to rush, cut the wrong topics and overwhelm those listening. Ruthlessly pick your playlist and stick to it.
- **Go out with a bang:** DJs always go out with a bang by saving their best tune until last to leave their audience euphoric. Never end a talk with questions. End with your final message and make it memorable. It's what people will remember most.
- **Use technology that works:** Guetta had perfectly timed streamers shooting over the crowd, dramatic light shows and eye-catching video screens. Nothing was delayed owing to technical failures, no reboots were needed. This is the number-one distraction for internal company presentations and talks. Get technology that works reliably, test it ahead of time and have a technical expert at the ready.

You may not have your audience dancing and waving with their hands in the air like Guetta does, but these tips will allow you to catch their attention, hold it and be well remembered.

Dance in the right direction

I was once out for dinner with an executive team midway through running their Digital Transformation Strategy retreat. I heard an announcement that frankly scared the living daylights out of me, and I tried not to let it show on my face! 'The line dancing lesson will start in five minutes.'

Watching line dancing is hypnotic, and these dancers were experts. After being persuaded, I reluctantly joined the chief finance officer and the chief technology officer on the dance floor, ready and willing to learn. It seemed that the teacher suddenly sped up her pace and complexity as soon as we stepped out. For the next 20 minutes, she shouted confusing phrases like 'applejack', 'anklerock' and 'fan kick'. I spent most of the time moving right when everyone was moving left and facing the back of the room when everyone else was facing forward. So I quickly left the floor. It was a sharp reminder for me of how it feels to be at the bottom rung of the learning ladder. I hadn't mastered it as quickly as I hoped and I wished the teacher would slow down. I wanted to practice the steps to the music, not learn more steps, and I ultimately just gave up.

I spent most of the time moving right when everyone was moving left

It is another example of how music can teach us just how difficult it is to follow along, especially when others are so far ahead of you. This happens when creative leaders are trying to follow along as their technology counterparts are explaining their technical challenges, or when the finance team is diving deep on the financial implications of a new product launch. It is time to consider what changes you are trying to drive in your organization and whether you are paying attention to who's dancing in time to your tune.

Accelerating effective communication

The CMO of Verve, Julie Bernard, has two brilliant approaches that accelerate effective communication with anyone. She developed these over the last decade as a marketing executive at Macy's, Saks Fifth Avenue, and now as chief marketing officer. In a recent interview she shared her two crucial practices for accelerating effective communication with her technology and business counterparts.

The 15-minute daily marketing and IT meeting

The first sounds so simple, but is incredibly effective. Julie holds a 15-minute meeting with the chief information officer every single day. Here she describes just how it works:

> Every morning I have a 15-minute meeting with the head of technology, always a phone call, never a Slack or instant message chat. The purpose is to check in and ensure all is going to plan, that everything is ok, that the team is on track. It is an opportunity for me to understand what I can be doing – anything on my end that can be done to overcome hurdles and remove organizational and/ or barriers that are getting in the way of progress. Since so many of my goals are tied to receiving support from the technology teams, it is critical to stay close to them and make sure we are collaborative, cooperative and, overall, watching each other's back. My team will never ever hear me say, 'The technology team is terrible,' or that the IT support is appalling. I always emphasize that if they have an issue, they need to be specific so we can resolve it. I am a big believer in upholding the team as a whole and positioning our tech partners honorably. It's a classic example of the principle of the Golden Rule, 'Treat others as you would wish to be treated yourself', and when you do so, they will return the same productive, healthy behavior.

The reason this works for Julie is that she is implementing what I call Powerful Preemptive Communication. This saves ten times the amount of time it would have taken otherwise. I love the simplicity of Julie's connection and the ultimate dedication to building the relationship between the technology and marketing teams and taking away friction, as explained more in Chapter 7 with the Innovation Trifecta.

The Three Email Rule

Julie not only has a concept for this, but she has proven over a decade that it works in a variety of companies. This rule simply speeds up resolution of what in some companies requires endless reply-all threads of never-ending backwards and forwards repetition. I wish I had met Julie sooner and I could have implemented this during my corporate life at Amazon and Microsoft. I could have impacted billions of dollars in productivity gains.

Julie explains how it works: 'I speak with people, not to people. Unfortunately, I believe too many hide behind technology, whether that be email, Slack or some other internal communication tool. My goal is to eliminate that bad behavior by employing what I call my Three Email Rule. When I hire someone new and am in the process of onboarding, I share the guardrails and explain that I will enforce it with a vengeance:

- **Email One:** The first email is the originating party communicating information to an intended recipient with a carbon copy to approximately 20 other people as a classic case of CYA.
- **Email Two:** The intended recipient writes back and, too often, these second emails reflect negative energy owing to some misunderstanding. Perhaps the individual doesn't intend to come across as negative, yet terse replies can be misinterpreted.
- **Email Three:** Then the originator writes back, either concluding the issue (a good thing) or with increased negative energy since they're frustrated that the second party "didn't get" what they thought was so clearly communicated in email one.

'My team knows at this moment that they should get up from their desk and go speak to the second party and resolve the communication issue in person (or via a good ol' fashioned phone call if the other party is remote). You have a calm, productive conversation and then the only appropriate use for the fourth email is for the first party and second party together to document and tell everybody else the conclusion to a productive path forward. That's it. Maximum four emails and the last one is for clarification and alignment only. My team will say that they pity the person who clicks "send" on the fourth email if that email isn't simply communicating the conclusion and closing the thread.'

The appeal of Julie's approach is the pragmatic simplicity of it. It is the sort of innovation Google needs to put into gmail or Microsoft needs to add to Outlook – on that fourth reply to a thread you could have a pop-up efficiency reminder saying, 'Are you sure you want to reply, why not just pick up the phone?' As the technology is not yet available, Julie's team are her own enforcers for the maximum four email rule.

Julie has a final way that she ensures this is not just a passing fad; at the end of every day, she counts emails like a store owner used to count their stock to check the number of sales. Julie counts email threads to see how productive her team has been. This counting will help teach her team new habits, which may include going to a team member to help them resolve an issue face-to-face rather than contributing to a 17-email thread of endless back and forth.

Julie has a very candid and direct style of communicating with anyone. My research shows me that this is not always typical and holds leaders back at all levels. In my work I often gather feedback for the executives that I am working with: I talk to board members, investors, executives and the teams they manage. Some companies call this 360 degree feedback. Frankly this sort of feedback has a bad reputation for a number of reasons. Firstly, the biggest problem with these exercises is that people focus on numbers and ratings, where people are trying to decide whether to rate someone a three or a four on a subjective rating. This loses the importance of the actual feedback you want to give and receive. Secondly, too often companies use this process as a delay tactic, or a mechanism to hide behind when an executive is not performing as expected, so a company can associate 'getting feedback' as a pre-emptive move for getting fired.

Sharing actionable feedback

The right way to use this feedback is not to spin everyone into an endless state of data confusion and useless metrics where nothing changes, but to gain relevant feedback that is immediately actionable given the context of the business and what is ahead, whether you are in high growth, manic mergers, turning around a business, planning for CEO succession, launching new products or expanding internationally. These are the factors that influence what feedback you capture and how you gather and share insights from that feedback.

When I launched my own company six years ago I used my research carried out in over 2,000 executive feedback sessions over two decades in global companies to create the *Context Sensitive Feedback*. I've found this approach to be powerful and useful, and it creates immediate insights and change.

There's one powerful question I ask that can actually be used in any situation where you don't feel as though you are getting to the heart of the matter: 'But what do you really want to say?' Despite all of my preparation with executives, many hold back the direct feedback they really want to give an individual. Here's what I often say to them: 'If you are hesitant telling me, then I am guessing you haven't told the individual involved and that is the very person who can most benefit from hearing exactly what you think!'

Boldly ask for what you want

Ask yourself questions like these:

- If you were being really bold, what budget increase would you ask for next fiscal year?
- If you were being really bold, what strategic initiative do you believe you should own?
- If you were being really bold, what would you ask your boss about your next possible career move?

Three executives I am working with surprised themselves when they got to lead an acquisition, received support for a 22 per cent increase in their headcount, and had a promotion brought forward 12 months, giving them a new title and compensation package on the spot.

Growing up in England, my mother always used to say to me, 'If you don't ask, you don't get.' Same is true in business. Are you boldly asking for what you want, or are you discounting your ask before you have even attempted it?

Every word counts

I was speaking at Gartner's Evanta Chief Information Officers' Executive Summit in Denver in 2019 and a CIO asked what was the best way to talk to a board member he was flying to see the following week. He told me some of the questions he was going to ask, and my response was one I give my clients several times daily: 'Instead of saying that, try this...' I provided a script, precise questions to ask and exact phrases to use. My approach basically boils down to 'purpose, preparation and practice' or what I call the three Principles of Words That Just Work:

1 First, this executive had to understand the purpose of this conversation, so I asked him: 'What do you want to get out of this?' Stating your intent or purpose at the start of

conversations helps everyone. 'I want to understand how and when you prefer to be kept informed' was the intent for this CIO.

2 Next, you have to prepare. Many executives run from one meeting, product launch, customer conversation to the next without taking a moment to plan what they are going to say and how they will say it.

3 Finally, what this CIO got to do was practice exactly what he was going to say. This gives you a chance to not stumble, consider if your intent is clear, and to hear alternative ways of saying it. One client got to practice a conversation in preparation for a one-to-one with her divisional president. She was frustrated that the promises during her hiring for promotion were not being fulfilled as fast as she hoped. She practiced, had the conversation, and the following week was told she was doubling the size of her team. Why this mattered most was her president was going on sabbatical and had she not had the conversation, it would never have happened for at least six months.

My favorite part of speaking is the audience conversation. It's why I'm not on the stage. I'm in the audience with my talks. I want to hear the reactions and questions and most of them are around how to approach conversations and situations. After my two talks with Evanta, the overwhelming feedback I heard was that it was powerful to take time to stop and think using approaches that can rapidly impact your business. Are you ready for what you really want to say and how you will say it?

What you want to ask your boss but are too afraid to ask

I often ask executives that I am working with, 'What do you wish you could ask your boss right now?' Too often we wait until the right time, the perfect time or a later time, when in fact you should ask it right now, today. Because everything changes quickly. Your boss gets promoted, your company gets acquired, or people who have the power to control your future have the wrong narrative about who you are, what you are doing, and how they can best help you. Here is a small selection of the questions my clients have asked their boss and the results gained. These are the types of questions that usually just remain in our heads:

Question:
'I am used to working in a much more empowered place. I need to hire who I want when I want, with the financial freedom to make investment decisions appropriate to my business responsibilities. I am ready to take on more. When can that happen?'

Results:
The following week my client had her responsibilities doubled right before top leadership changes. Had she not had this conversation when she did, she would have had to wait at least a further six months before any possibility of consideration for a promotion.

Question:
'I love this company, but the headhunters are calling and I'm beginning to understand my strong external worth. I'd love you to consider evaluating how I am compensated relative to the business results I am achieving.'

Results:
When this executive's company declined to address his compensation concerns, it helped him realize that his *External Personal Stock Valuation* as described in Chapter 1 was significantly higher than his *Internal Personal Stock Valuation* and shortly after he landed in a new company with a more senior role and 27 per cent higher compensation.

Question:

'I'm noticing ideas for us to hit our growth goals fall between various functional teams. What we need is to pull together a cross section of creative, technical and business brains to explore innovation possibilities. Can I lead making that happen?'

Results:

My client is now leading an Innovation Trifecta Accelerator Program with my help to unlock possibilities across their global divisions and functions. Without asking, those ideas would just be sitting in the depths of people's brains or endless ignored to-do lists.

Question:

'I would love a conversation about what I need to do or demonstrate that will improve the probability of me becoming vice president. When is a good time to have that conversation?'

Results:

Their boss was able to articulate that it wasn't about the results they were achieving, but about the visibility of those results to people that mattered. That is what the executive is now working on to improve the probability that he will be promoted.

Question:

'It occurred to me that in my effort to help out, I may have come across as overbearing and getting too involved in your function. Is that how I have come across to you? My intention here is to identify opportunities for us as a company to save money so that we can reinvest it. How can I best help you with that?'

Results:

These two executives now have a new level of transparency and candid conversations and are working together more closely than ever to identify how to tap into each other's expertise for the greater benefit of the company.

Question:

'My questions are: I want to know how you are so successful while my regions are lagging behind; how can I get a better understanding of that?'

Results:

Once my client had asked this, his interactions were far more productive and his peers began volunteering more information and became more open to sharing ideas with him.

Your boss or peers cannot answer the question in your head. Say it out loud and find out what is possible. If you end up hearing a truth that you don't want to hear, then at least you can focus on your next possibilities. You can start collating your own phrases and Words That Just Work and save them for when you may need to reuse them. Or perhaps you are thinking of a scenario where you would love the perfect words to say.

BONUS FEATURE

As a special bonus for every reader, I offer you a complimentary Words That Just Work for your situation. You can text me by entering in your cell phone number at www.textvalnow.com. You will receive a message back saying I have received your number. Let me know your name and then you can text me your situation and the results you want to achieve. I will provide you with *Words that Will Just Work*.

By now you may have realized that you need to perfect your questioning techniques. You can learn a lot from watching masters at work. Babs Rangaiah is one of those with brilliant questioning skills.

Ask better questions

Seven times. Seven times he asked his precise question in seven different ways. I was at the Digital Ascendant Executive event where Babs Rangaiah, executive partner of global marketing at IBM, was in deep conversation on stage with another executive. The first time he asked his question, it was part of another question so it could possibly have been missed. The second time he asked his question, the other executive used it as an opportunity to tell a related story, a great diverting tactic taught by many who receive media training! The third time he asked his question he gave two options: 'Was it this or that?' (He was getting closer.)

The interview continued. So did Babs. Each time he referred back to his original question he asked it in a slightly different way, increasing the vagueness and providing the other executive freedom to share what he was willing to. On the seventh attempt we all got to hear exactly what we wanted. It was impressive.

I can't share exactly the topic that was revealed, as it is confidential, but it doesn't dilute the lesson. Babs told me afterwards: 'As long as your persistence is greater than their resistance you'll win.'

This is a critical lesson in extracting what you need from any interaction. Of course, style matters and the way you ask will improve the probability that you will get the answer you are looking for. But my guess is that many of you are giving up too soon to ask for precisely what you want. Here's another proven way to get what you want fast.

How to use fewer results for greater results

If a CMO of a complex global $10 billion-plus company can write their strategy on one page, why can't you? One of the executives I am working with created a paper placemat for her CEO to review her new strategy. All on one page. It enabled her to get her new three-year plan approved in record time, and allowed the executive team to consume her new strategy at the right level without getting lost in the details. She did it by using the following Executive Team Communication Rules.

If a CMO of a complex global $10 billion-plus company can write their strategy on one page, why can't you?

Ten rules for communicating to your executive team and board:

1 Start with the headline first. Your audience will ask you for the detail they need next.
2 Do not use a 125-page deck to convey your message.
3 Speak at the right altitude for your audience.
4 Provide your point of recommendation, not your endless debate.
5 Be clear on the intent of your conversation and state it to prevent crossed wires.
6 Don't use a paragraph when a sentence will do.
7 Don't use a sentence when one word will do.
8 Don't use a word when silence will do.
9 Preview key recommendations one-to-one before communicating topics of importance.
10 Recap and summarize what will happen next before the meeting ends.

If you follow these guidelines you will improve your influence at the executive level, but it also requires your ability to deliver an impactful presentation.

Brilliant presentation

I have spoken at over 200 conferences in the last five years, and in the process I have got to watch other executives present.

Unfortunately, it is not always pretty or productive. If only conference organizers offered speaking coaching to those who presented, if only more companies would see the value of teaching their executives the power of being up on stage, if only executives could see that it is fairly easy to rapidly change the impact you have on stage by how you tell stories and engage your audience. If only.

Not only do I speak at many conferences each year, I also work with executives to prepare them to be brilliant on stage at internal company events and external industry conferences. You don't get to shout, '*Cut! Take two*' for a live performance. That is what Michael Bay may have wished for when he panicked and walked off stage at a Consumer Electronics Show in January 2014. Many watching thought it was ridiculous that this famous Hollywood director could not improvise and talk about Samsung's new curved TV when his teleprompter failed, yet stage fright is more common than you think.

Being a dynamic, provocative speaker can increase your influence, improve the probability of your idea being accepted, and enhance your reputation as a leader in your team, company and industry. Working with leaders in all industries, I have seen good, bad and downright cringe-worthy presentations. I want to share 14 Crucial Communication Tips for Creating a Memorable Presentation that you might even enjoy giving:

1 **Create a memorable beginning and a dramatic end** to capture attention and leave the audience with a provocative thought. This means you do not apologize, complain, tell a joke or do a sound check.
2 **Ditch the slides!** You do not need them. Jared Carstensen, CISO at RCH, used five letters in his closing keynote at Gartners Chief Information Security Officers' Executive Summit. I'm a fan of being concise and his presentation was perfect. He had five letters, A, B, C, D and E, on five slides and shared a lesson for each letter. It was memorable and the audience focused on what he was saying, not complex PowerPoint slides.

3　Tell contagious stories that prompt others to tell their stories. I often tell the story about how one of my CEO clients increased their share price by 37 per cent in the first three months of her appointment. That prompts others to tell me stories of success or not such great success during their first three months in their new executive role.

4　Decide what happens next. Consider what you want your audience to do differently after they have heard you. Make sure your content leads them there.

5　Share the one crucial takeaway you want the audience to remember and build your talk around that.

6　Tell a story about why you are passionate about your topic. Consider what got you excited, or talk about how it has impacted you personally.

7　Always leave time for people to share reactions, commentary, disagreements and questions.

8　Adjust your style to your audience and consider the crucial information you want them to hear today, not everything you could possibly tell them.

9　Don't pretend to be someone you are not. I am from England, and Europeans present differently from Americans. You won't get any whooping and high-fives from me; it just doesn't work and I am not being authentic if I try.

10　Video yourself to practice, then listen and try it without your notes.

11　Talk to the contrarian: *'Before you think I am stuck in a time warp suggesting that…, let me tell you this story….'*

12　Get your audience to reflect, learn and think with you.

13　Be ready for the unexpected. Prepare for the lights to break, your time to be cut, the format to be changed, and be ready to go with the flow.

14　Be brilliant at sharing your brilliance. What are you most proud of, and how often do you tell the stories of your accomplishments? Too often we hold back, don't want to appear to be bragging, or opt for being humble when our brilliance will truly help others.

As you hear others speak, here are some questions to ask yourself:

- Are you enthralled or rolling your eyes?
- Are you distracted by your phone or mesmerized?
- Do you feel like someone is reading your mind and explaining just how you feel or do you think they are from another planet?

Most importantly, ask this: do you immediately know what you are going to do next?

Radiant Communications Circle

Many leaders ask me for inspiration when communicating beyond email. The Radiant Communications Circle (Figure 5.2) is designed to provide you with a plethora of options. You can pick any one of the 20 rays of communication and implement them immediately. The key is not to be polished. Don't perfect it, speed works far better than your fourth edit that delays it 24 hours or more.

Here are two very specific examples of how the Radiant Communications Circle works in action.

FIGURE 5.2 The Radiant Communications Circle

VIDEO IS WORTH A MILLION WORDS

If a picture is worth a thousand words, a video is worth one million. Of course, I can't show you a video in this book, but let's put this to the test. If I try to describe to you in infinite detail the dolphin I saw jumping the waves in Newport Beach one summer, you may have an idea of what I saw. Perhaps if you have seen a dolphin close up you will understand my excitement, but maybe not. Even a picture would help, but until you see the video, you can't truly experience it for yourself. Yet we try and describe information, context and ideas to our work colleagues via email all of the time. How are you letting your team experience what you are seeing and thinking? If you go to www.rapidgrowthdoneright.com you will see the dolphin video example there, and then perhaps you will have a better understanding of what I experienced.

REVIEW A MOVIE

When I talk to leaders about how their emotions impact their work, I encourage them to watch Disney's *Inside Out*. Once they get over the shock that I am suggesting they could learn something from a children's cartoon, they are surprised by the movie's impact – not least in helping them perfect their poker face and not let anyone see their disgust when in disagreement with someone else, as many times leaders don't articulate their disgust in words and barely avoid a teenage eye-roll at the end just to underline their disgust! You can get the Anger, Disgust and Sadness Movie Team Discussion Guide at www.rapidgrowthdoneright.com. What movie have you watched recently that you can take lessons from and apply to your team?

CHAPTER 5 RAPID RECAP

1   Which of the Radiant Communications can you try with your team today?

2   Ask your team to bring a photo of their favorite piece of art and what it means to them.

---

3   Ask the aspiring artists in your company to submit works of art to decorate your walls.

4   Make the most of your eight seconds of attention.

5   Ask yourself how much of your intended message creates understanding and belief.

6   Consider how others' brains work differently from yours.

7   Tell stories using music as the catalyst.

8   Implement the Three Email Rule.

9   Who could you benefit from having a 15-minute daily meeting with?

10   Notice and remember the Words That Just Work for you in getting results.

Now that we have explored many new ways to create influence by communicating creatively, we will look at how you can rapidly make decisions.

Endnotes

1   Rahim, Zamira (October, 2018) Banksy reveals how Sotheby's shredding stunt went wrong, *Independent*, https://www.independent.co.uk/arts-entertainment/art/news/banksy-girl-with-balloon-sothebys-auction-video-wrong-auction-art-a8589461.html (archived at https://perma.cc/K7FJ-Z3VF)

2   Mercuri, Monica (July, 2019) The World's Highest-Paid DJs 2019: The Chainsmokers topple Calvin Harris with $46 million, *Forbes*, https://www.forbes.com/sites/monicamercuri/2019/07/29/the-worlds-highest-paid-djs-of-2019/#291bb7887a97 (archived at https://perma.cc/R4C9-N57C)

How to speed up decision-making

In my work with executives around the world, I have seen that the number one cause of dissatisfaction about the speed of business growth and innovation is focused on how decisions are made. Technical, creative and business minds approach decision-making from different angles; the key is not to conform to one set approach. By creating disruptive disagreements with clear boundaries, decisions are faster, stickier and allow for rapid innovation. This chapter includes practical exercises and case studies that will give pragmatic guidance on how to eliminate the decision dilemma holding back innovation. The first step is knowing how you typically make decisions at work and then mapping how your fellow creative, technical and business peers make decisions.

CHAPTER TOPICS

- The creative, technical, and business decision dilemma
- The bamboo effect
- Evaluating speed

FIGURE 6.1 Rapid Growth Decision Dilemma

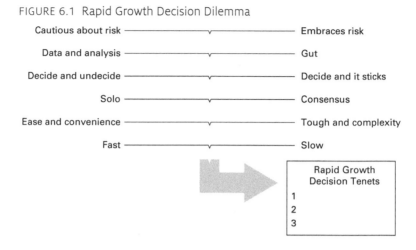

The creative, technical and business decision dilemma

One of the greatest causes of frustrations is confusion over decisions. You think the decision is yours to make, but your peer wants final veto, or decisions are made that impact you but you don't have input, or perhaps there is an illusion of inclusion when the decision has already been made. Or maybe you believe that decisions are clear and not a cause of confusion with your team. You can use this chapter to explore with your team and peers where there is room for improvement.

Think back to when you last made a major business decision, like funding a new initiative: how did you make that decision? Did you gather data, analysis and dive deep into the numbers? Did you know instinctively what you were going to do and sought to validate that with opinions? Were you swayed by others or did you make it alone? Did you take the time you needed or make a fast decision? Were you presented with new information but stuck to your decision or did you adapt? Did you keep your decision to yourself and make it on your own, or did you consult other people you trusted?

How you make similarly scaled decisions is unlikely to change, and you are unlikely to change the decision-making preference of your team, your boss and your peers. The crucial step is understanding others and reaching an agreement on how you will make collective decisions. That is where many leaders fail. I created the Rapid Growth Decision Dilemma tool (Figure 6.1) to remove the spin and uncertainty that can suck away hours of time and energy.

You can plot yourself on the Rapid Growth Decision Dilemma along with your significant peers in the creative, technical and business space and see how you need to adapt to help others get to decisions faster. You can also create Project or Company Decision Tenets to unlock capacity in your company to make decisions faster.

I have completed this exercise with hundreds of executives, and every time their response is the same: 'Now I understand why decisions are so confusing around here, and it is so easy to solve.' In my work I find that many executives wish they didn't have to make so many decisions and the people who work for them wish they could have more empowerment. The solution is a systematic way to understand, provide clarity and take action to change the decision-making habits of your business. Chapter 11 reinforces how to make those changes stick, but first let's pause and apply this to your current role right now by completing a review of your current decisions.

Try this exercise:

1 Create three columns on a piece of paper.
2 Under the first column list decisions you wish your boss would let you make versus needing to consult with them.
3 Then, under the second column, list decisions for which you are confused about who owns what, who cares about them and who needs to be involved.
4 Finally, use the third column to identify decisions you are currently making that you want to give to someone else. This could be on your team or in another function.

This will unlock great capacity for you personally and for your team, because we fall into common patterns and habits and don't always stop to think if this is the best use of time. Once you have completed your Deliberate Your Decisions table (found in Table 6.1), you then can work through what changes you can make to rapidly increase decision-making in your company. Ask your team and your peers to complete it, and you will create the same clarity you get when you finally have your windows cleaned – you will wonder how you were ever able to see clearly before! Your role in leading rapid growth is to create remarkable decision-makers around you.

Your role in leading rapid growth is to create remarkable decision-makers around you.

I heard nutrition guru Robb Wolf speak once and he offered a surprising piece of parenting advice that equally applies to leading rapidly growing companies: *You need to raise good decision-makers. Because your kids will make the most impactful decisions when you are not there.*

His words didn't just apply to teaching your children to eat well, nor did they just apply to parenting. They equally apply to leading teams. You have to teach your team to make good decisions when you are not around.

TABLE 6.1 Deliberate Your Decisions

Decisions you want to own	Decisions that are unclear	Decisions you want to delegate

That is where the power of Rapid Growth Success Soundbites comes in. Soundbites are echoes that continue when you are not there, like footprints in the sand that show your team where you are heading. If you are intentional about how you set them, they can create and guide your team into becoming a group of brilliant decision-makers.

Rapid Growth Success Soundbites

To accelerate decisions you have to help your team lead when you are not in the room. You need to set your soundbites so others know what you want them to do when you are not there and to guide them through every step of the way.

Julie Bernard, chief marketing officer at Verve, has three Rapid Growth Success Soundbites:

- Just say yes.
- Champions adjust.
- Love your base players.

Perhaps you can guess what the meaning is for each of them, which is the true power of a soundbite, but I'll let Julie provide more detail in her own words about how these have become the foundation of her success as a chief marketing officer:

JUST SAY YES
'This equally applies to my own career as well as how I want my team to approach their work. Throughout my non-linear, untraditional career I've developed broad experience by exposing myself to a variety of different roles, guided by a philosophy of "Just say yes". I've led various groups across different business silos. Anytime I was approached by my boss or one of their peers asking me to take a different role, I would simply say, "Yes, OK, I'll try it." I was in merchandising when I was asked: "Will you join our planning division?" I moved into planning, then I was approached: "Will you join corporate strategy in finance?" I was in finance and was asked, "Will you lead our vendor relations

group?" Next I was asked, "Will you take over this particular technology work?" Shortly afterwards, they said, "Will you take over the process re-engineering work?" From there my moves continued across warehouse management, client relationships, consulting, customer strategy and marketing. Especially early in my career, I was fortunate to have advocates who trusted me and believed in my strengths more than I knew myself; with their encouragement I would just say yes, even if it was something where I had no prior experience. I often thought, well, if they believe in me, I am confident that I will figure it out just through perseverance, asking thoughtful and intentional questions, collaborating with others, empowering my team and good old-fashioned research. As a result of these challenging yet fulfilling experiences, at this point in my career I don't see myself narrowly defined as a marketing executive. Rather I characterize myself as a dependable strategy executive who can leverage this fortuitous broad strategic and operational experience; I've actually performed the jobs I talk about, ranging from customer experience to marketing, advertising, merchandising, product, supply chain and tech. "Say yes" is definitely one of the important ones. Don't overthink it. Know that you can do it. We always can.'

CHAMPIONS ADJUST

Julie's second soundbite relates to how she wants her team to lead through change, which she always says is at the heart of many of her previous roles. She explains more: 'Adaptability and flexibility is critical for me. It was a former colleague who first captured my fixation on this idea: "champions adjust". I really do bring it up daily; the essence of it is that we should never hold ourselves captive to the gravitational pull of prior thoughts, opinions or approaches. If new information, new data, new perspectives or new contexts present themselves and they inform you and advance your thinking, then you have to be willing, open and courageous enough to change your mind and adapt to that change in an action-oriented way. I like to say go and get it done, thoroughly and fast. Too often we get married to our ideas and we don't recognize that maybe that idea is no longer relevant or right because context changes.'

ALWAYS LOVE YOUR BASE PLAYERS

Julie's third soundbite was born when she kept using baseball analogies with her team: 'I love the baseball analogy, and I talk about how I am building my own baseball team – people with different strengths and experiences – so that someday when I start my own business, I would have people that could play the different bases I needed. Over time I started to realize that hiring and developing teams is not about just building the team. It is about thoughtfully filling the bases, yes, of course, with smart, hard-working, curious people, and then empowering them to play their base. Yet more importantly, I found that when I have had the best teams, it's because I sincerely love and respect them as people who are doing the best that they can. That is where I always show my team loyalty.'

It is important not just to have Success Soundbites but to make sure that your team can see them in practice and how they influence the way you and your team make decisions. Julie was able to show this in reality: 'It is easy to talk in platitudes about being loyal to your team. Too often I bear witness to colleagues who throw their own team members under the bus for their own advancement or as an excuse when something goes wrong. Across many industries you hear executives speaking about customer loyalty, with leaders discussing tactics such as loyalty programs as a mechanic for customers to prove their loyalty to them. Instead, we should be thinking about how we, as business leaders, show our loyalty to customers, to our clients. Similarly, I started to apply this approach to myself as a leader, recognizing that we need to "show loyalty to our people". For me, responsibility is my badge of honor. I think about my responsibility to be loyal to my team. In my role as their leader or their manager, it is my responsibility to be their advocate. I take this role very seriously. As I have always been leading change initiatives and innovation initiatives, there is a degree of career risk for the people who join my teams; if we're not successful, if I don't set them up for being successful when they are playing their base, they could lose their job, which is a serious situation and a possibility that I do not take lightly. I come back to my high responsibility quotient. They have families to support, mortgages, car loans, college fees, retirement dreams, whatever it is. When I personalize my commitment to them, focus on raising them up, spending time with them, and bringing them into the loop and truly coach, develop and train them, they perform, you perform, and teams truly do win. Love your base players. Hire them right upfront, let them play their base and always really love and respect them in doing so.'

Julie epitomizes doing the right thing when no one else is watching. That is how you want your team to make decisions.

The bamboo effect

How's your calendar looking right now? Does it have the open space you require? We have a gardener who visits our house weekly to trim the crazy bamboo fence we have around our back garden. If we don't prune weekly, the bamboo shoots up from every tiny opening and soon it takes over, suffocating every living thing in its path. The same applies to meetings. They take over if you don't pay attention, spreading fast and taking over your days and weeks.

When I ask executives what the number one thief of time is, meetings is always the answer. These are often pointless, futile, self-aggrandizing, time-wasting spectator sports that suck the living energy from companies.

Sometimes it is the fundamentals we forget. I'm not likely to be going to tell you anything new or groundbreaking here, but if you implement these concepts, you will free yourself and your team to focus on your big, bold goals. If you are the CEO, this is as easy to fix as clicking your fingers. If you are a divisional, functional or other leader further down the organization chart, it will take some influence by osmosis, but it is not an impossible task. The greatest key to the success is discipline and follow through. This isn't about perfect meeting checklists during meetings, nor will it require any training or workshops. But it will require an acknowledgement of your current meeting reality and a united desire to change and improve.

When I speak at conferences or coach executive teams, I often tell leaders I can immediately eliminate 75 per cent of their meetings by using this premise: half of all *Half of all meetings are not needed.* meetings are not needed. Of those meetings that are needed, only half of the people attending are needed. My maths may be overly simplistic, but this provides you with 75 per cent of your time back to use as you choose.

There are three reasons leaders don't fix their inefficient meetings:

- **FOMO (fear of missing out).** Ever since the elimination of personal assistants taking minutes and circulating them and the lack of good documentation, too many people fear being left in the lurch if they don't attend a meeting; they worry that they will miss out on an update, lose a battle with a peer or not be present to influence someone important.
- **The helicopter boss.** It isn't helicopter parents you have to fear, but helicopter bosses. They insist on having every meeting on their calendar in case they want to drop in or still attend debates and decisions that they need to be freeing their team to make in their absence.
- **Using culture as an excuse.** That's the way we/my CEO/my board likes to work isn't a reason to never consider other ways of working.

Perfecting your 'perfect meetings'

Once you've addressed the reasons for so many meetings, follow the Before, During and After rules for 'perfecting your perfect meetings':

Before

1 Is a meeting even needed or can two of you just decide?
2 Who needs to be there for input/debate/decisions?
3 What specific outcomes do we want to achieve?
4 If we were being concise, how long would we need?
5 What context, data or insights will attendees need?
6 What is the right format for the meeting?
7 How will I best prepare and share my input, written brief, summary, context articles or background?
8 Who needs to know about the outcome but not attend?
9 Does this have to be in person or will phone/video be as effective?
10 What is the time allocation for each topic?

During

1 Start with allocating a note-taker and a clock-watcher.
2 Write the outcomes and time allocation where everyone can see it live or virtually.
3 Jointly silently read any background or narratives.
4 Allow everyone time for input and debate.
5 The decision-maker decides.
6 Repeat through all topics.
7 Agree about next steps and timing.
8 Decide if /who/when another meeting is needed.
9 Recap decisions and actions.
10 Close when outcomes are all achieved.

After

1 Circulate notes and actions to attendees and those impacted.
2 Ask for feedback on the perfect meeting from attendees.
3 Schedule in your calendar time to act on the actions you collected.

Here are more steps to take to perfect 'perfect meetings' in your company:

1 First, imagine all of your current and future meetings evaporate. Nothing is sacred, nothing continues in its past form.
2 Note the key future goals of your products, services and company targets.
3 Ask yourself who needs to gather, why and with what frequency or duration to deliver those goals.
4 If you were inviting the minimum number of people possible to decide/debate/inform, what would that look like?
5 Set a 'perfecting your perfect meetings' review for one month from today.
6 Record a video explaining why you are making the changes you are making and what people can expect.
7 Finally, note how many total hours you have given yourself and your team by perfecting your perfect meetings.

This is the sort of initiative that seems great when you hear someone at a conference talking about the efficiencies to gain, and you likely head-nodded your way through this chapter, agreeing with the craziness of the inefficient companies you have worked at in the past or today. But the most rewarding part compels when you apply discipline and consistency to implementing it for your teams.

- **Immediate insights for your business**
  - If you are not the CEO, what allies can you co-opt to help you reduce your meeting time by 75 per cent?
  - If you are the CEO how can you co-opt the board to embrace this approach for your strategy planning and board meetings?
  - If you were to roughly estimate how many hours you could save for your division or team, what would it be?
- **Immediate insights for you**
  - Consider your calendar and it is likely you will want to add connections and time for the output of Chapter 1's Influence Bullseye target.

- Which meetings that you own can you immediately cancel, cull attendees from or clarify the purpose of?
- Create a reset and relaunch your new ways of working for your team.

- **Immediate insights for your team**

  - Consider who on your team needs/wants more frequent connection and FaceTime and who is more independent/ who you can set free.
  - Ask your team how they can proactively reset their own meetings and decisions.
  - Encourage your team to track hours saved to reinforce the benefit of the new way of working.

Evaluating speed

The 10 am/2 pm decision test

The ultimate test of an efficient decision is to take the 10 am/2 pm test. Can you make a decision at 10 am and implement it by 2 pm the same day? This is easier in smaller companies, but not impossible in larger companies if you set the right decision-making tenets. Partners at law firms, accounting firms and family-owned businesses may have a broader level of influence they have to exert before they can implement decisions. This requires a strength of Influence Bullseye from Chapter 1 that mirrors a large company because of the ownership structure.

Can you make a decision at 10 am and implement it by 2 pm the same day?

One partner shared the reality of the 10 am/2 pm test: 'It doesn't necessarily work that fast in my world. In the business that I run, there are three other partners to influence before we can make a decision. If I were to go to a conference and hear a new idea, then I would have to take it back to them, talk it through, convince them that this was a good decision, and that this was the way we wanted to go. Sometimes we talk about a new initiative for months or years before we are ready to implement. It just takes a little more of a rallying effort and getting everybody on the same page and moving in the same direction. It's a bigger ship to turn for new decisions, even though we are relatively small.

If you make a decision at 10 am, how long is it before it is implemented? To speed up decision-making, you have to look at both the elapsed time to make a decision, and also the annual cycle of how and when decisions are made.

Your annual cycle of decisions

Skip to Chapter 11 to determine where strategic decisions are made in your annual rhythm. To speed up decisions to the right pace, you need to consider what altitude of decisions you are responsible for and how that fits into the overall company timing of strategic planning and corporate goal-setting.

You will have peaks and troughs of preparing for, influencing, making and then executing decisions, depending on your annual calendar. You may be used to a very structured and static annual cycle, or if you have recently been through three unexpected acquisitions in the last 18 months (as one of my clients has), then your annual cycle of decisions could be flexing so frequently that you may feel like you are freefalling without a parachute! Just as important as decision-making season is the quiet season for decision-making, which is often over the summer months between product launches and your company events.

Your decision downtime season

Summer is simply magical. Even though it often starts with the rush of graduations, school musical performances and the like, come June or July, the magic of summer arrives with lazy mornings, exciting travels, new adventures and memories that you will retell for the next several decades. Or does it?

Does your company have a downtime season for decisions and execution? It may vary by division if you work across different industries and market segments.

Perhaps you dread summer starting because of the plans to be made, school being out and the crazy camp schedules and kid entertainment options, or the family reunions you would rather not attend? Many people dread it for those reasons.

Ask these three critical questions each summer or during your own company downtime season:

- What impact do you want to have made in your whole life, not just your work life?
- What memories do you want to create with friends and family?
- Consider the next five summers. Where do you want to travel to visit relatives or take your kids before they head off to college?

Here are some ideas for how to make the most of your decision downtime season:

- Summer is the perfect time to reset how you make decisions with your team.
- Summer is the perfect time to reset how involved you are with your team. My bet is they want you to be LESS involved than you are today, saving you hours.
- Summer is the perfect time for trying something new. This past summer, I dared to try real camping (not even glamping, real camping) and I completely surprised myself and I didn't hate it! Now it is part of our new family summer tradition.
- Summer is the perfect time for creative projects. I have a CEO client who has just decided to start painting again after a decade hiatus. Not all decisions have to be work-related.
- Summer is the perfect time to give back and adopt a new cause as a family.

- Summer is the perfect time to try new ways of living. We have 'boss days' where in turn a daughter is the boss for the day. She decides everything that day from where we go, what we do, what and when we eat, and what happens when arguments happen. It's highly entertaining and incredibly freeing not to have to parent for a day! Some of my clients implement this idea in their teams, allowing a team member to make the decisions for a day.

What can you plan to experiment with every summer? Returning from downtime season is also a crucial moment for a decision reset. Here are three ways to do just that:

- **Celebrate beginnings, not just endings**
  When my eldest daughter moved into second grade and only two of her friends were in the same class, she asked where all her friends had gone and she wanted to start a new holiday celebration called Friends Day. Right then we started a new tradition where at the start of every school year we would invite the whole class and their families to our house to allow the children to play while the adults got to say hello to each other. Too often we have parties that celebrate the end rather than the beginning. We have parties when employees leave, projects end and bosses move on, when really you reap far more benefits by having a celebration at the very start. Celebrate the beginning of a new project or the return of your planning or budgeting season and put a positive spin on decisions that sometimes pull a team down.
- **Reset the view on the horizon**
  One leader I worked with regularly used pictures from his vacation to share new insights with his team about how he was thinking about the future business horizon. Are you telling inspiring stories to your team about where you see your business going in the future? How can you capture this and share it when you return to work?

- **Remember adults hate routine change too**
  Habits easily form that make people miserable. It is sometimes easier to keep saying yes to commitments. Ruthlessly attack your calendar and chop out time-sucks. While changes of routines are hard, use this time of year to reflect on which routines are working for you and which you want to change.

You control your routines and how decisions are made more than you realize. Don't let them control you.

Decision lessons for start-ups

Amazon is often cited as best in class for how they make decisions and run meetings. I spoke with a former Amazon executive and VP of Strategy at Ideo, Andrea Leigh, about how she filtered what to leave behind and what to bring to Ideo, a rapidly growing start-up.

> Since so many of our leadership team came from Amazon, we thought hard about this. There were things we loved and didn't love about Amazon's culture – things we felt helped them to be effective, and also things we felt held them back. We kept the Dive Deep, Think Big, Customer Focus and Bias for Action principles which are critical in an agency environment. We left behind Amazon's internally competitive culture. In an agency environment, this works against you. Everyone needs to be on the same team and pitch in to deliver for the client. We also added the 'would I have a drink with this person?' test. Being personable and having strong relationship-development skills are critical in our environment, while at Amazon it was more important to be right and possibly less well-liked and that significantly impacted how decisions were made.

If you were to evaluate all the companies and teams you have worked on, which parts would you take with you and which would you leave behind? You have greater influence on how decisions are made when you are growing rapidly than you may realize.

CHAPTER 6 RAPID RECAP

1 Encourage the freedom of saying yes.

2 Create your Rapid Growth Success Soundbites to guide decisions in your absence.

3 Unlock your Rapid Growth Decision Dilemma with your peers.

4 Guide your team to know to adjust with today's reality, not yesterday's.

5 'Perfect your perfect meetings' and give your team back precious time.

6 Work with your peers to reduce your meeting-time investment.

7 Experiment with making a decision at 10am and implementing it by 2pm.

8 Identify and make the most of your decision downtime season.

9 Celebrate beginnings, not just endings, to reinforce change.

10 Be empathetic to the pain of change.

CHAPTER SEVEN

How to increase the quantity and quality of ideas

There is a reason that 'location, location, location' is a popular phrase in buying and selling homes; it is the crux of the valuation and has a unique multiplying factor that can take a home from $100,000 to millions purely based on its zip code or postcode. The same applies to the 'location' of coming up with new ideas. In this chapter we'll find out how to rapidly uncover new ideas that may well lead to your next billion-dollar project.

CHAPTER TOPICS
- The intersection of venue and innovation
- The Rapid Growth Innovation Design Experience
- Your Rapid Idea Generator

The intersection of venue and innovation

Nobody ever gets their best creative ideas in a drab windowless conference room, yet companies around the world are having meetings right now in places that quite frankly suck the energy and ideas out of the very people they are looking to inspire.

While you may not be able to immediately influence the location of your headquarters or even style of your current offices, paying attention to where you host your regular team meetings or your quarterly strategic retreats will make an incredible difference. Remember how you feel when you visit a restaurant with a fabulous view, inspiring decor and uplifting music. Your mood immediately changes and you relax. Leaders who pay attention to the location of their meetings get greater ideas from their teams and reduce the probability of the collective eye-roll of frustration and attendees reaching for their phone for an alternative distraction.

Here are five of the best and worst places to generate new ideas:

Worst:

- your regular windowless conference room;
- a corner of your open-plan office where interruptions are continuous;
- a meeting room where you can be interrupted;
- your own cramped office;
- any untested failed video-conferencing solutions that just don't work.

Best:

- anywhere that is a break from your normal work environment;
- private dining rooms in restaurants with a view;
- meeting rooms in libraries, museums and art galleries (Seattle Library and the Seattle Sculpture Park have some amazing spaces);
- luxury car show rooms (yes, they rent them out for private events);

- PeerSpace offers unusual venues for rent for corporate events that include lofts, train carriages and theatres.

Innovation happens when you are outside of your comfort zone. What can you try that is new for your next team gathering?

What is innovation?

Too many people get stuck on the definition, scope and purpose of innovation. Given I am an innovation expert, you are probably expecting me to give you my definition and defend it against all previous definitions that have come before. But I am far more pragmatic than that and don't want to distract your focus on growing your company with an intellectual debate about the meaning of innovation. If any executive I work with truly needs and desires a clear definition (which is rare), we create one specific to their customers, strategy and long-term goals. For the purposes of this book, let's focus on how to increase the quantity and quality of ideas, because it is ideas that lead to innovation.

Ideas for ideas' sake are a bit like going for a walk without considering your destination, including how you will get there or why you want to go there in the first place. It might be mildly entertaining, but won't produce any significant results. That is what I see with many company innovation efforts. You need to start with a Big Bold Goal. Xbox certainly needed a Big Bold Goal when I was working with their leadership team shortly after Nintendo launched the Wii. On Wii you could play tennis on your TV with a controller attached to the TV with a wire and pretend to swipe the controller to return each serve.

Ideas for ideas' sake are a bit like going for a walk without considering your destination.

New ideas blossom from a billion-dollar disaster

We immediately chose the right location when Xbox needed to come up with new ideas. It was a painful time to be on the leadership team at Xbox, part of the Entertainment and Devices division at Microsoft. Hardware failures had caused the infamous 'red ring of death' to flash on the front of consoles, rendering the gaming console useless: we opted to replace every faulty device while we uncovered the issue, and this resulted in a $1 billion write-off that led Microsoft's then CEO, Steve Ballmer, to seriously question if the division should be shut down. The pressure was on to create something new and innovative. I worked with the Xbox leadership team to create the equivalent of an Innovation Lab ten years before innovation labs even had a name or became popular. I have since used this approach with companies across all sectors and created a toolkit that will increase your quality and quantity of ideas: the Rapid Growth Innovation Design Experience.

The Rapid Growth Innovation Design Experience

Using the Rapid Growth Innovation Design Experience, you, too, could create your next multimillion-dollar idea or your own *Guinness Book of World Records* award. Table 7.1 provides the ten-step process, and using Xbox as an example, you can learn how to apply each step with a product that went from idea to execution in rapid time. The first germ of an idea came from the Xbox Kinect and this design experience became known as 'the. best.offsite.ever'.

TABLE 7.1 The Rapid Growth Innovation Design Experience

	Questions to consider
1 Location	• Choose a surprising, unusual or unexpected location.
2 Attendees	• Invite creative, technical and business minds. • No ego invites. • Invite international perspectives. • Consider which partners should join.

(continued)

TABLE 7.1 (Continued)

	Questions to consider
3 Design	• Centered around a Big Bold Innovation Idea. • Be aware of the roller coaster of energy.
4 Inspiration	• Prepare attendees prior to the meeting. • Innovative journey. • Immersion in customers' lives.
5 Idea Explosion	• Create environments for unlimited ideas. • Allow for creative freedom. • Incorporate non-linear thinking. • Appeal to all types of learning and thinking.
6 Filtering	• Allow for crazy ideas. • Create ideas to compete.
7 Pitching	• Select your decision-makers. • Break corporate rules. • Prepare for the debrief.
8 Funding	• Have funding ready for the winners. • Allocate discretionary resources for new products and services.
9 Reality	• Prepare for the reality of implementation. • Designate time to plan for scoping, budgeting and resourcing the implementation phases.
10 Reflection	• Capture key learning at the design, approval, planning and implementation phases.

- **Location**

  We chose a collection of cabins in Leavenworth, a sleepy village a couple of hours north of Seattle where there was no internet connection (this mattered over a decade ago). We asked for all chairs to be removed and replaced with sofas and comfy seating.

- **Attendees**

  We intentionally annoyed a lot of executives who wanted to join. We did not succumb to the ego invite – where just because you invite one VP, you have to invite three of their peers. We selected attendees based on their unique perspectives, bringing in a range of creative, technical and business experts from around the world, not just those in the US.

- **Design**

The multi-day event was designed with our overall Big Bold Innovation Idea in mind: 'How do we broaden the appeal of the Xbox?' We paid particular attention to the roller coaster of energy that naturally happens in any event to make sure we took the attendees on a journey of peaks and troughs of energy and involvement. We also decided to break every cultural norm at Microsoft at the time: we banned spreadsheets, financial analysis and PowerPoint. We had artists capturing ideas visually, Lego, Play-Doh and creative tools for representing ideas.

- **Inspiration**

We started the inspiration before the event even began, with an immersion into the future targeted customer that we wanted to reach – articles, videos and challenges were shared beforehand. As the attendees boarded the bus to the event, they were given a goody bag filled with the kind of magazines and products that our new customers would typically have, and we played video clips on the bus ride to help share what our target customer listened to, cared about, read, and where they spent their current precious social and entertainment time that we wanted them to spend with Xbox.

- **Idea explosion**

This is the part that many mistakenly spend all of their time and energy on when coming up with new ideas, but it is only a small part of a complete program and you need all of the other elements in place to uncover the ideas that will transform your business. You also have to use sophisticated techniques that will appeal to all kinds of learning and thinking, because just as we discovered in Chapter 5, not everyone's brain works like yours. You need to create idea-generating methodologies that will appeal to everyone.

- **Filtering**
  We divided attendees into small groups and they were able to select their favorite ideas for a science-fair-type exploration of possible ideas. During the walk-through of the exhibitions, you couldn't critique an idea, only add to it. Some teams spontaneously combined their innovation and created a new combined idea. We led a thumbs-up thumbs-down voting session that narrowed the ideas down to the top five to be worked on further to ready for the pitch session with the executive review panel. One of the most popular ideas – that of controlling your Xbox with your voice and by waving your hands – emerged when software, hardware, marketing and design members got together and realized that this was not just a technological dream, but a distinct possibility.

- **Pitching**
  If the panel to whom you pitch your new idea has not been involved in the innovation experience, it is essential that you prepare them well. This is because they can squash the germ of an idea before it is fully developed. With 'the.best.offsite' ever, we had to prepare the pitch panel to realize that there would be no financials, no spreadsheets, no pretty, over-the-top PowerPoint presentations. What we wanted them to pay attention to was the possibilities, the idea, the customer experience and whether each idea could not only beat Nintendo Wii, but reposition Xbox away from the shooting and racing hardcore gaming device it was known for, so that it could become the center of the living-room entertainment device we were aiming for. The winning bid went on to become Project Natal, and launched as the Kinect Camera for the Xbox 360 gaming console in 2010.

- **Funding**
  After winning the pitch, a small team was rapidly funded, and that team went from 8, to 50, to 200 at speed.

- **Reality**
  The innovation story never ends with the initial idea. Persuading a large, global, complex organization like Microsoft to understand and believe in a new direction was no simple feat. Especially as we were now targeting a broader audience, one that no longer simply liked to shoot and race things, which, frankly, was representative of the majority of Xbox employees of the time. So the first task was to make sure we had the right voices designing, creating and building this new product for new customers, and not everyone was delirious about it.
- **Reflection**
  Before you get too caught up in the excitement of implementation, it's wise to rapidly capture reflections and key learnings at the point you move to execution. This is the most valuable part for any future innovation experiences, and it is imperative that you capture and share.

The Kinect Camera launched in 2010 and sold 10 million devices in three months, making it the fastest-selling consumer electronics device of all time and earning a place in *The Guinness Book of World Records*. While the Kinect may no longer be in production, its technology is now used in many Microsoft products. Its greatest impact has been in the medical field, enabling doctors to use simple hand gestures to change, move or zoom in on CT scans, MRIs and other medical images to make surgery faster and more accurate.

The Kinect Camera launched in 2010 and sold 10 million devices in three months, making it the fastest-selling consumer electronics device of all time.

Before you start creating your own Rapid Growth Innovation Design Experience, consider the following questions that will prevent you from making common mistakes.

Questions to ask before your offsite or team event

Any offsite or team event can either be eye-rolling-inducing or the very point that galvanizes your team and makes a difference to real business results. These questions will help you assess this ahead of time:

- What business outcomes do you want to achieve by the end of the event? (Teambuilding is not a business outcome!)
- Is the team I am inviting the one that will be with me in six months? Delay it if you have significant changes coming to your team.
- Do you know whether your team understands your strategy, believes in your strategy and knows what it is getting in the way of achieving your business results?

Not all Big Bold Goals are immediately clear. Sometimes you have to discover what is missing before you eventually refine your Big Bold Goal to create what is truly important to you. That is just what a two-star Michelin chef did in Los Angeles.

Innovation lessons from a Japanese entrepreneur and chef

Imagine being at a restaurant for the fourth time and you are served a menu uniquely created for you. Imagine that the chef of that restaurant knew more about your tastes and what you would like to eat that night than perhaps you do yourself. What if that chef remembered exactly what you ate the previous three visits, and had hand-selected a 13-course menu just for you. Imagine if that chef didn't just do that for you, but for each and every one of the 26 guests also dining at the restaurant that night?

You don't have to imagine, but you do have to travel to Los Angeles, and patiently wait to get a table. The story of how Japanese chef Niki Nakayama created n/naka contains many important lessons in innovation. This wasn't Niki Nakayama's first restaurant venture. She had opened a sushi restaurant before, but she had not perfected the 'trifecta of success'. This trifecta of considering the creative, technical and business elements of an idea was fueling Nakayama's frustration. The restaurant was technically outstanding, serving perfect sushi with perfect rice, at the perfect temperature, with the same food for everyone. She had hit all of her business metrics, yet she was not fulfilled because she was unable to unleash her creative expression, so she sold her business. She had checked two out of the three elements of the trifecta – the business and technical aspects – but because the creative part was missing, she was dissatisfied and not achieving what she had hoped.

When you sell a company, decide to seek funding, consider an acquisition or make a large career decision, you need to take a *Selfish Wallowing Holiday*. Ideally a SWH lasts for weeks, but it can be measured in days; sadly, many dedicate less than a few hours to it.

Niki Nakayama had dreams of her SWH being at home in comfortable clothes and growing her hair very long, and ordering pizza. But within days, while she was listening to US radio station NPR about a story on chef's tables, she had a spark of an idea that awoke her creative passion. After all of her formal training in Japan, in other restaurants under expert chefs and in her own first sushi restaurant, she found her creative outlet – creating her very own unique restaurant where she could craft her own inimitable experience, where she could cook whatever she wanted to cook, however she wanted to cook it, just the way she wanted it.

SHATTERING THE EXPECTATION AND EXPERIENCE FOR CUSTOMERS

History teaches us what to expect. Experience becomes predictable, habits form and we all know what to expect from a typical restaurant experience. Nakayama wanted to change all of that. One of her dishes is called *shiizakana*, which essentially translates as 'not bound by tradition', or chef's choice, which truly epitomizes Nakayama herself.

She openly shares how, growing up in a traditional Japanese family, women were not expected to reach high levels. Women were expected to be supporting characters in men's lives. Her brother was given the family business to run, and Nakayama wanted to prove she could do something different. She trained under many great chefs, where she was often the only woman in a kitchen full of male chefs, and that is where her determination grew. When someone puts you down or says you can't do something, your will to prove them wrong grows. Nakayama had this burning desire to prove all those who doubted her wrong. She allowed her food to be bold, loud and make dramatic egotistical statements: her food could be everything that she wasn't comfortable being. One of her favorite Japanese words is *kuyeshe*, which essentially means 'Screw you, watch me'. The culinary world was doing just that: watching Niki Nakayama when she was awarded the coveted two Michelin stars for n/naka in 2019. Her restaurant continues to be booked out three months ahead of time, with new reservations being released at 10 am each Sunday for the following three months.

Whenever you eat at n/naka, Nakayama and her team know exactly what you ate last time and every time before it. They then prepare something completely unique for you. This insight and personalization is both remarkable and simplistic, beautifully wrapped up together. Many companies could easily replicate it, because data is collected endlessly, but rarely used for such impact.

Let's use jetBlue as an example. They are one of my favorite airlines to travel with and their mint first-class service is delightful, not least because several of their seats have an elongated desk feature that makes working mid-flight incredible. I often pick a different flight time just so I can get one of the coveted seats with the desk, because it is where I can write free of distractions. However, the one disappointment with jetBlue is that every time I board and I am welcomed at my seat, I am asked the ridiculous question 'Have you flown with our mint service before?' This is where my polite British heritage takes over and I smile and say, 'Yes, many times,' when I secretly want to scream 'YES, you have the data, you can check my mosaic frequent-flyer profile. You can see that this is my tenth flight this year with jetBlue!' I know enough about technology to realize that flagging my previous flights and informing the inflight cabin crew might be complex, but imagine what experience it would create for some of their most profitable customers.

- **Idea instigators for your business:**
  - Do you know everything you could about your customers' past spending and interactions with your company?
  - What could you do if you were crafting a highly customized product, service or experience for your very best customers?
  - You might have the data on your customers' behavior and spending, but can your creative, technical and business teams easily access it? How could you make this easier?
  - What is your industry's equivalent of the Michelin Star Awards? Do their values connect with yours and what do you need to do to achieve that external validation and recognition?
- **Idea instigators for you:**
  - Ever felt like Niki Nakayama? Are you in a role where you might be successful but not satisfied? Check whether you are achieving your creative, technical and business needs for your perfect role; revisit that assessment in Chapter 2. Maybe a critical element of your Perfect Job North Star is the creative outlet, or perhaps the technology challenge or the business impact you are making – or perhaps all three.
- **Idea instigators for your team:**
  - If you were to guess, how many of your team might be feeling like Niki Nakayama? When you watch them can you tell they are excited, energized and in their perfect job?
  - If you were having conversations with your team members about their perfect job, what observations or insights would you share?

Just as Nakayama reinvented the restaurant experience, the hotel industry is finally being disrupted and new innovation is occurring.

Reinventing hotels

Have you ever been to a hotel where you can choose precisely what time you check in and check out? Have you ever asked yourself why no one has invented that? Perhaps when you arrive at a hotel after a long journey, you are hungry or thirsty, but before reaching for the minibar you make the mistake of looking at the price for the minibar items. Now you might be asking yourself if you really need that $11 bottle of water or that $12 packet of nuts. I have often wondered whether the labor cost of stocking and restocking a minibar justifies the 1000 per cent markup on water, snacks and drinks. Why don't they charge a reasonable price? It's crazy. What about when you're in a hotel and you are sat in the lobby dialing into your third conference call of the day, and you would really love a cup of coffee – but you can't possibly go and get it. Wouldn't it be great if someone could just bring it to you?

I often wondered why nobody had ever tried to solve these issues. That was until I stayed at the Virgin Hotel in Chicago where they had not only solved the 'pick-your-own check-in and check-out time', but the room-service issue. You can order from their room service menu and they will come and find you anywhere in the hotel and personally deliver it to you. They have launched and maintained some really innovative services for their guests, disrupting a market of sameness in a way that hasn't ever been done before.

Here are five ways in which Virgin Hotels have created an innovative hotel experience:

- **Gathering your data and actually using it**
  As you book, you are asked very specific questions about what would make your day if you found your favorite snack in your minibar. I've completed these kinds of questionnaires before, but never so specifically, and never has a company actually used it. Upon arrival in my room (or chamber, as Virgin calls them), I found a handwritten welcome card on my bed along with a packet of my favorite crisps and a Cadbury chocolate bar.

- **A minibar at grocery store prices**
  Virgin broke the high-profit-margin con. At Virgin Hotels, the items in the minibar cost what it would cost you at your local grocery store.
- **Doors**
  Design matters, and design for the woman traveler matters even more. I didn't realize I needed doors within my hotel room until I stayed elsewhere. Virgin undertook research that showed that women travelers valued privacy and more of an apartment feel to a hotel room, rather than one big open room. Having doors solved that challenge, especially when ordering room service.
- **Allowing you to choose your own arrival and departure time**
  You can let the hotel know when you will be arriving and when you would like to depart, all from their mobile app, and they will adapt your stay accordingly. This app can also control the temperature and TV in your room.
- **Providing food and drinks anywhere in the hotel**
  This sounds so simple, and I don't know why other hotels haven't tried this sooner or copied them since. You can order a full menu and have it delivered anywhere in the hotel – on their rooftop bar, in their library or in their common rooms – at any time of the day. Perfect for the jet-lagged business traveler.

The Virgin Hotels experience blew me away. There is another hotel that we can learn from that also found unique ways to surprise and delight me as a customer. This was on a break to Santa Barbara with just one of my three daughters. I've checked into thousands of hotels, and for the first time ever, as we walked into the lobby we were greeted with something I had never heard before. 'Please take a seat and I will check you in,' the receptionist called out to us. So simple – yet surprising. The receptionist walked over to us and introduced herself as

Virgin Hotels and Hotel Californian give a lot of thought to the customer experience.

Chantelle, and she then told us all about the recently renovated hotel while we sat on a squishy sofa. A pure delight.

A week later, when we returned home, a surprise package arrived for my daughter, Olivia. It was a thank-you note from the General Manager Warren Nocon and a gift of a child's-size bathrobe. Olivia had written a thank-you letter while we were staying and we were both surprised and delighted that he took the time not only to reply, but to send her a perfect child-size gift. Virgin Hotels and Hotel Californian give a lot of thought to the customer experience. Now that you have two more ideas of how to surprise and delight your customers, you can consider how to apply them to your own business.

- **Idea instigators for your business:**
  - What are some traditional ways that your industry serves its customers that are ripe for turning on their head?
  - What exorbitant costs do you charge your customers that, if reduced, would differentiate you from your competition?
  - What boundaries of delivery do you currently face and how could you break them down?
  - Who in your industry is disrupting delivery models, pricing structures or customer satisfaction that you can investigate?
- **Idea instigators for you:**
  - Have you had a Virgin Hotels-like service experience that you can share with your team?
  - How do you thank and reward your team in unique ways that would surprise them?
- **Idea instigators for your team:**
  - How are you regularly capturing ideas of surprise and delight that your team experience? And how do you share those across your whole team?

Disrupting the fitness industry

Peloton launched onto the stock market in 2019 with a valuation of $8 billion, which was double its private valuation from 12 months prior. The hype has been immense, although cynics say Peloton is just a bike with an iPad attached. The innovation runs far deeper than that.

Here's why Peloton is so unique and the envy of many businesses:

- They give customers ultimate freedom on how to consume their products – live class or recorded; 15-, 30-, 45- or 60-minute duration; hip hop, country, or live DJ; low intensity or intervals – the choices seem endless.
- Its instructors have become stars. Take a look at Ally Love or Alex Toussaint's social followings and you'll see Peloton is making stars out of their instructors. Taking care of and nurturing long-term relationships is a big risk for Peloton, as the instructors are becoming as strong individually as the collective brand.
- The statistics and leaderboards are addictive. I nearly fell off my bike when my friend in Palo Alto started Face-Timing me while I was on my first ride as the Peloton team were setting up my bike in my house. Whether you compete or not, knowing which rides your friends have completed and following a program with a community around the world create a stickiness like no other fitness experience.
- The company creates a strong community by using #hashtags so you can identify people in your city, age group or with similar interests to ride with.
- It has a raving fan base. It has multiple Peloton Facebook groups with members in the 100,000s. As a frequent traveler, I was delighted to find a Facebook group set up solely to help people book hotels and airbnbs that have Pelotons. I've even seen members allowing other members to come to their house to share their bike so they don't lose their unbroken ride streak.
- Century Ride T-shirts. Do your customers crave swag that shows off how often they use your products? Peloton sends riders a Century Ride T-shirt celebrating their 100th ride. They are coveted treasures, as proven by those who have purchased them on eBay for as much as $150,000.

The commercial that launched their holiday 2019 campaign, in which a husband purchases a Peloton bike for his wife, was extensively criticized for its unhealthy depiction of body image and marriage. The reaction to this from Aviation Gin was a brilliant example of a rapid idea well executed. The Peloton wife, actress Monica Ruiz, was seen drinking Aviation Gin with her girlfriends, celebrating leaving her husband. As Aviation Gin investor and actor Ryan Reynolds told TV host Jimmy Fallon on his TV show *Tonight*, they were able to track the actress down and within 36 hours of finding her were able to shoot, edit and release the sequel commercial. Now that is how you rapidly grow your business in the right way.

With the last three examples, I immersed you in innovative experiences and asked you questions to encourage you to consider how these apply to your business. This is what I call Immersive Inquisitive Innovation, in which you go and visit, study or learn about another innovation that could be similar, operating in parallel or completely disconnected from your company and industry, and then seek to apply these to your own business.

Generating ideas is only half of rapid growth done right; implementing them at scale is the toughest part. That's where we will turn our attention next.

Five lessons from Mars

Gulrez Arora, head of Mars Seeds of Change Accelerator and Global Leader of Digital Innovation at Mars, implemented the Innovation Trifecta in multiple ways across Mars.

THE POWER OF THE INNOVATION TRIFECTA

Gulrez evaluates all of his innovation initiatives against criteria of desirability, viability and feasibility. Figure 7.1 shows how this maps to the Innovation Trifecta where creative, technical and business approaches overlap. Mars launched an innovative campaign for Maltesers chocolates in Australia for Easter where

FIGURE 7.1 The Innovation Trifecta evaluation

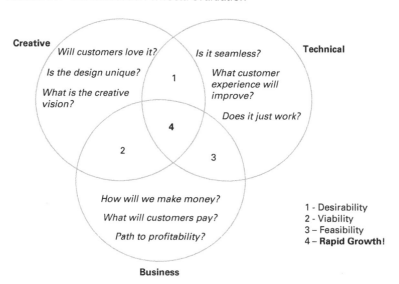

they teamed up with UK-based geolocation company What3words to create an immersive combined online and real-life treasure hunt in a search for the missing Malteser chocolate bunnies.

What3words is an innovative company in themselves, as they are changing the way we record and notify our locations. They have divided the world into 3-meter-by-3-meter squares and have named every single one with three unique words. Their goal is to make it easier for emergency services, travelers and businesses to rapidly find each other. Gulrez used What3words to create a digital treasure hunt to win a $5,000 reward.

I asked Gulrez why the Innovation Trifecta was so crucial to his campaign success and he shared this with me:

What I call desirability is if a customer wants it, and you have to connect with the customer on an emotional level. You have to ask: Does the consumer like it? Does a consumer want it? And I think creativity plays a critical role here. I work in a crowded space. We live in a world where there are many competitors, there are lots of delicious products out there. Therefore, it is really crucial how you resonate with the consumer, and how you tell that story and connect with the consumer at an emotional level. The power of creativity and technology gives us the experience that will test if they are willing to spend $2 on your product. At the heart of this, nothing is possible if you don't make money. You can be the best storyteller, but you have to convert fast. That is the business component that you have to be able to easily evaluate and test. New technologies like the What3words location-based service allows you to be even more creative and to really expand how we engage with our customers. Our message can now be delivered in a much more immersive experience and in a far more personalized way – the consumer can really touch and feel it. The final feasibility test is to ask these questions: is it sustainable? Does the technology work? Can we deliver those huge pieces of content and can we utilize it across various channels in a way that it will work and allow us to make money?

You can be the best storyteller, but you have to convert fast.

BE CLEAR ON THE CRUCIAL MEASURES OF SUCCESS

You have to set clear measures of success for any innovation initiative. Here are the measures of success for the Maltesers Easter Bunny campaign:

- **Feasibility:** We had to ask whether it worked end-to-end seamlessly for the consumer. Everyone who interacted with the campaign was able to attempt to crack the clues using the geolocations to find the chocolate bunnies.
- **Desirability:** Did we hit our engagement targets with how people followed, participated and interacted with the campaign?
- **Viability:** We sold more Maltesers, which helped us see that we had a campaign that we could scale to other products and regions.

You can view a video of the campaign on www.rapidgrowth doneright.com or view your own three-word location at www. what3words.com. What possibilities does the What3words experience conjure up for your business?

SUCCESS BREEDS SUCCESS

Gulrez explains how success breeds success: 'Creating, proving and executing on a concept builds your credibility, which then allows you to go out and get a few more initiatives funded. It is almost like creating a bridge fund that allows you to fund future executions that you can move forward at a greater scale.' I see this happen as more new products go to market and have positive feedback, confidence and therefore future funding increases.

Particularly in decentralized companies like Mars, crowdsourcing initial ideas strengthens support for the ideas that eventually get funded. Gulrez has noticed the ideas that come from crowdsourcing have a stronger internal backing from Mars executives and a larger probability of success. 'Really, the true superstars of the program are the forty associates, brand managers and market leaders that raise their hand, write the brief and participate in the program. Finding those champions in regions around the world allows for more incubations.'

INFLUENCING WITHOUT AUTHORITY TAKES PILOTS TO WIDE-SCALE IMPLEMENTATION

Having a network of influencers as described in Chapter 1 with your Influence Bullseye is one crucial way to accelerate the impact of innovation trials in a more organic grassroots upwards method. The stronger the leader is at building a group of executive supporters, the higher the volume and speed that innovations are incorporated.

A VISIBLE AND POWERFUL CHAMPION

Often overlooked, the strength of a powerful champion accelerates any innovation effort. The Seeds of Change launchpad at Mars has chairman Stephan Badger as the sponsor, which immediately puts the program at the right altitude and priority for all those involved. As the Global Leader of this program, Gulrez agrees: 'It adds a whole other level of intentionality that Mars is saying yes, we want to create a world where there is better food for everybody. With our chairman engaged with the program and helping us judge and pick those participating, it is first-class. It gives a whole different gravitas to the program, both internally, externally, and even for the companies that are in the accelerator. We have seen this in intangible and in measurable ways, in marketing, PR and start of the recognition of the programs and the quality of the applicants that applied to the program.'

Your Rapid Idea Generator

The chief information officer at Belkin, Lance Ralls, wanted to bring his global IT team together to increase the results and impact that his technology team had on the company. I am not a fan of monotonous offsites and feel that fluffy team-building is a complete waste of time. So when I do work with a client to bring their leadership team and whole organization together, it becomes far more than just another meeting.

We didn't quite realize at the time just how much this global team would find value in coming together to understand the business and create a greater belief in the future strategy of the business. Several told us they were considering other job opportunities but were now back 'all-in'. This alone saved half a million dollars, and that is not counting the additional revenue-generating ideas that were created that day.

A few weeks prior to the meeting, Lance's team completed the Innovation Inventory Assessment from Chapter 4, and as part of the event we completed a Rapid Idea Generator, where we created the ability to review the results and suggest immediate changes that would improve the probability of the team hitting their goals. Within a couple of hours, we had over ten ideas that would increase sales, save costs and increase the level of service provided. Here's some specific feedback from attendees:

- 'I finally got to put faces to pictures of people I have worked with for the last five years, and it was very helpful. When I first joined the company I was excited, I wanted to take on the world. Over the years, not seeing people, not coming over here or people coming to see me, it started to get very lonely. I felt isolated, nobody knew what I did. This year was really difficult, a lot of companies were contacting me to work for them, I had my doubts, and having colleagues was really important to me. It feels like I just started here and it is my first day. So now I want to do great things again. This wasn't how I felt coming here. I am going to reboot myself.'

- 'We usually have updates and announcements. Today we had to think, we could pitch our ideas and it was thought-provoking. I feel motivated. Now I am going to go back and implement some of the ideas for my team and for myself personally. I now know what my soundbites are so I can lead my team better.'
- 'Great to ideate and hear from the US and regions and joining us together which will help us create results as a leadership team.'

When did you last bring your team together face-to-face? You need to orientate them so that they have their gaze in the right place.

The right horizon

I used to stand on the beach and gaze across the sea and see Steep Holm and Flat Holm islands millions of miles away – or at least they seemed to be to me, as a small child standing on the beach-front at the quaint English seaside resort of Weston-super-Mare. Many of my friends had traveled in Europe and across the ocean to the giddy heights of New York and Florida. I would thrive on their stories and pictures of their adventures, imagining the possibilities beyond what I had seen for myself.

I used to stand on the beach and gaze across the sea and see Steep Holm and Flat Holm islands millions of miles away.

I am currently fascinated by *Black Mirror*, the Channel 4 TV show on Netflix that is set in the future. It is just far enough in the future to be understandable and believable. It pushes your thinking of how current artificial intelligence, social media or virtual reality could impact how we live. In one episode you see a world where every human interaction is given a star rating of one to five and how that rating impacts your financial and social standing. It is frighteningly just a little too believable and brilliantly made.

'You aren't thinking big enough,' is a phrase I have found myself saying to several of the executives I am advising. Sometimes you can't see the possibilities when you are so close to your work and the impact you are having on your company, your industry and your community. Visual clues, extreme extrapolations and surrounding yourself with external advisers who challenge you will expand your horizon and help you see the possibilities beyond your current thinking.

Before attempting to create new ideas with your team, ask yourself whether you are looking far enough out on your horizon and how can you set the right view for your team.

The remarkable power of Kickstarter

If you are looking for ideas and inspiration, browse Kickstarter, Indiegogo or other crowdfunding platforms that have opened up access to funding and unleashed a flood of new and innovative ideas and businesses. I spoke to Shane Small, Executive Creative Director of Snapchat and Facebook, formerly of Xbox, Hulu and WizKids and one of the three founders of the card game Exploding Kittens. Exploding Kittens, the number-one-backed Kickstarter of all time, was backed by 219,382 people in its initial campaign. It is every entrepreneur's wildest dream – to hit your goal and achieve 1 million dollars of backing in just a few hours. The campaign ended up raising $8,782,571 and broke many Kickstarter records.

Companies have to realize that anyone can launch a Kickstarter for funding ideas, so if you are not tapping into the creative genius of your people, they might well go and do it for themselves.

Shane shared how he joined forces with Elan Lee, former chief design officer at Xbox Entertainment Studios, and The Oatmeal cartoonist Matt Inman to create a card version of Russian roulette, with exploding kittens, unicorn pigs and a strange combination of a taco and a cat called tacocat.

Here are six innovation secrets from the highest-backed Kickstarter campaign:

- **Boredom triggers innovation**
  'We were bored; we kept asking what we could do that was different. I originally had the idea as a digital app but then thought how we could make it out of cards. We knew it would be fun to play right now this very second, so we made the game out of a normal deck of cards. As more and more people started to play it, it became addictive and exciting to figure out the strategy and we knew we were on to something. It was originally called Bomb Squad and that didn't seem quite right. That is where Matt came in.'
- **Find people who are better than you**
  'When Elan and I met Matt Inman we instantly knew he could bring something very different to our idea. Although art and design are my passion, I am always looking for people who are good where I am not. Matt brought a unique style and great ideas. He suggested kittens that exploded and we were hooked.'
- **Your competition can help you**
  'We love Cards Against Humanity and given their overwhelming success, we approached them to get their advice. Elan made the connection; they are amazing and have been incredibly supportive. We knew nothing about cards, other than from my time at WizKids. We needed to learn all about inventory, shipping and product supply, all of the reasons businesses fail. They have been fantastic helping us.'

- **It matters that you love what you are doing**
  'I love this game, I am so proud of it. I have never created a game that feels so fun and complete. I cannot wait for everyone to start playing it.'
- **Learn from your past mistakes**
  'I always have another idea in my head. My previous projects may not have been the commercial success I had hoped, but I have learned how each has had their different challenges, whether launching on the wrong platform, not picking the perfect time, or production challenges. Each one has made me proud, as I have paved the way for others to be innovative and I have learned to be tenacious and keep coming up with new ideas.'
- **Always create fun times**
  'With all the additional funding we will be able to create more expansion packs and have lots of new great ideas to share. We are going to see how far we can take this and how much fun we can create.'

Kinect came from a one-off innovation lab, Mars has an accelerator program and its own innovation lab, Virgin is disrupting the hotel industry by innovating as they expand, and Exploding Kittens used Kickstarter to rapidly test and fund a crazy idea for a card game that three friends had when they were bored. There are many paths to exploring, validating, testing and launching new ideas. Now you have several tools for how to identify, unlock and evaluate ideas in your company, next comes how you implement them, which we explore in Chapter 8.

CHAPTER 7 RAPID RECAP

1 Create an innovation lab.

2 Build an accelerator program.

3 Complete an internal crowdsourcing exercise for ideas.

4 Launch an external crowdfunding on Kickstarter.

---

5   Create a one-off innovation experience like Kinect.

6   Run a Rapid Idea Generator.

7   Reflect on innovative companies.

8   Paint a picture of the future and ask for paths to get there.

9   Visit another company for an out-of-the-box experience and debrief the lessons you learn and how it can apply to accelerate your vision.

10 Run a Hack-a-thon-style event.

11 Create a 'gather 1000 ideas' type process.

12 Challenge a creative insights initiative for alternative proposals.

13 Run a competition with grand prizes.

14 Create a Shark Tank/Dragons' Den experience.

15 Ask for a written submission of a perfect story.

16 Invite a group of high school students in to create solutions to your challenges.

17 Run a customer immersion event.

18 Create what-if scenario conversations.

How to work with a genius

You'll have at least one person in your company who is a *genius*. Quite possibly many more. By showing you how to set them free, this chapter provides a simple yet radical way to lead your expert technical and creative employees. It shares how companies often suffocate and hold back the very experts they need to create breakthrough thinking. With unexpected lessons and unusual approaches, you can break free from mundane norms and rules. It starts with how you define who you are as a company so that every genius and everyone else feel connected, inspired and included.

CHAPTER TOPICS

- Because we give a damn
- Managing your marketing genius
- Rapid Growth growing pains

Because we give a damn

Mark Essayian, president of KME Systems, 'gives a damn' about his customers and he uses that tag line in his conversations on his website, and lives it every day. The reason he uses such a direct explanation is because he really does care. When he was articulating his core values, he got lost in the double speak of marketing and was concerned he would sound like an idiot and it would not represent him or how much he cares about his customers. He told me:

'You know what? We give a damn. That is what is going on our website because it is true, despite some people telling me I couldn't say something so blunt. I reminded them it was my company and I can get away with it, running a business in Southern California, because it truly reflects how I feel about my customers and employees. Have I lost a customer or a prospect over it? Maybe, but I view it as self-selecting. They're not going to be a good fit for us.'

Sometimes you have to make sure your intent doesn't get lost in translation and it captures the essence of what you want to get across. Mark backs it up with how he supports his customers: 'It doesn't matter who I talk to. I can quickly explain what my company does: we provide IT services and we give a damn. If your phone system is down, it's like my own phone doesn't work. If your email is down, it's like my company email is broken. If you have a business problem, I have a business problem, because I give a damn. We used to just say, "We give a damn." But I learned the powerful impact of using the word "because" when influencing others.'

You need to break rules when working with creative leaders and teams.

Creativity at its finest

You need to break rules when working with creative leaders and teams. Taking them through your usual business processes might not only drive them crazy, but you will lose out on the very brilliance that you want for your whole business, not just your creative areas.

Here are five keys for success when leading creative teams:

- **Prepare to challenge your company norms**
  Depending on the size of your company, this may be either incredibly easy and fast to achieve or take a monumental act of influence. You first have to understand each as a unique individual. Cara Ely, VP of games at King, describes how she slowly gets to understand her creative team:

  > Being creative is a very personal act, so you have to make a personal connection with your team, to build the trust needed to take risks and innovate. There's not a one-size-fits-all option; it takes authenticity and communication, and can't be shoehorned in later on. Don't rush into action mode without understanding the people you're working with and how you can best come together to create something unforgettable.

- **Work backwards to work forwards**
  You will fast discover that creative people have ingenious ways of influencing others. Cara at King uses a Pre-mortem process with her technical and business peers:

  > In the early stage of every game, I do a Pre-mortem with our technical team where we imagine it is a year from now, and our project had failed miserably. What were the reasons? That discussion reveals so many potential pitfalls, interesting perspectives and hidden fears of the team. Then we can address them directly.

- **Your enthusiasm and energy are contagious either way**
  It is easy to spot someone disenfranchised or switched off. To inspire creative teams it is essential that you tap into and frequently share your positive enthusiasm for your project and ideas. Here's how Cara did that with a computer game she designed that became a seven-game hit series:

I designed and launched an original game based on wedding planning with a team of game developers who had absolutely no interest in the theme. We shipped in six months and it became the studio's most successful IP. We went on to make seven games in the series, and it's still active today. During development, I didn't downplay my enthusiasm. I knew the team was skeptical, but I believed our players would love it, so I communicated my optimism and passion as often as I possibly could (even when I had my own moments of doubt). Many games on the market at that time were rather dark and ominous, and our game was bright, beautiful and lighthearted. I focused on how different we were, how much the team's work would stand out in the market, and how we were paving the way together for something new.

- **Set the vision, and set your team free to deliver it**
  Cara's final words of wisdom are to set a clear vision and let your team take it from there:

  > Your job is not to know all the answers. If you have a clear vision, ask for help, and put trust in others to deliver on the creative goals, your idea will go places you never expected and never could have reached on your own.

- **Don't assume managing people is the ultimate goal for everyone**
  When I was working at the Rare Games Studio shortly after Microsoft had bought them for $375 million, I distinctly remember their art director enthusiastically talking about his love for sketching and character design and then he switched his gaze to the giant pile of paper on his desk, an endless stream of performance reviews and financial budgeting documents. I watched him physically slump as he gave a strong teenage eye-roll at his impending paperwork mountain. At that moment I knew we had to let him just draw. I soon discovered his reluctance to let go of the paperwork wasn't because he was good at it or loved it – quite the opposite – but because he was concerned it would affect his bonus and

potential to earn future salary increases. We quickly removed that as an issue, and that freed him up to do what he did best. We appointed someone who enjoyed and was good at the people-management aspect of running the art department and created a perfect match.

Sometimes you need to look further than your own company; you have to tap into your creative thinking about how you can have an impact on your broader community. That is what John Phillips did in his role as SVP of talent at Starbucks.

Breaking mundane rules to impact your results and your community

Starbucks launched an initiative to help 5.5 million of America's youth that were out of work, and John was part of the small team that saw an opportunity to broaden this to include other companies and make this a coalition that went broader than hiring at Starbucks. The initial goal was 100,000 real jobs offered to 18–24-year-olds; now the initiative is on track to provide 1 million jobs by 2021.

Sometimes you need a raw call to action, an emotional plea, a personal pledge and that is what John provided as he sat on the plane on his way back from the first careers fair that he and his team designed in 2015. That fair offered those first few jobs to the unemployed kids in Phoenix. Rather than try and summarize what he achieved, John allowed me to share his letter here:

> I am on the plane on the way back from the 100K opportunities fair and forum in Phoenix and I am struck with several emotions… Pride, sadness, excitement, fear and joy… and yes even anger (no, this post is not about the movie *Inside Out*). Some of those are expected when attending something as significant as an event that is about putting America's youth to work and offering them opportunities. There is a lot at stake. There is a lot to do and the divide in America is getting bigger not better.

But this post is not going to go into all the details of the event. You can see details here. It was an amazing display of what a group of companies can do when they work together for common good. It will be well documented and I implore you to read and learn more about the 5.5 million youth that are currently out of work and not in school. Staggering and not acceptable. But it gets worse because the problem is generational and what has been clear to me is that it is not about kids with a lack of skill. It is not that they are not motivated. It is not that they are sitting idle and want handouts. Those are the sensational stigmas that we assign because we need to assign blame to something and what an easy target but youth.

I am here to tell you that it has little to do with any of those things. I watch with my own eyes though the lens of talent-acquisition and human capital. My job is to win more than my share of the world's top talent for Starbucks. That is what my shareholders and company demands of me. But at Starbucks we do things through the lens of humanity. We constantly push ourselves to balance profit and social impact. I love it. But what I see in the opportunity campaign is extremely talented kids... young adults that have one thing in common. We, the leaders of America and the influencers of society, have crushed their spirits. We have given them every reason to doubt and no reasons to believe. We tell them NO you're not good enough, No you will never make it out of your upbringing. You have no chance because of the color of your skin or income class of your family. What I am witnessing firsthand at these events is the fracturing of the American dream. And I am angry, frustrated and even a little guilty that my path has allowed me privilege that I wish on everyone. With a family that backed me at every step and told me repeatedly that I WAS good enough and I can accomplish anything... when I struggled in school it was still YES you can. When I chose not to go to college they still believed in me. Enough so that I live life with a courage to take on anything and to follow my dreams. I was told YES.

That's all it takes. Say YES. Yes, you can, yes, you are fully able. Yes, you can overcome your circumstances. Yes, you can be the first in your family to achieve. Yes, you can change your life forever. YES.

The American dream is broken. And I am part of the problem because I have sat idle. But I can change too. I can choose to pass on the story of what I am seeing. I can say Yes to those that only hear no. I can be a light in a world that is gloomy. I can offer guidance when needed and I can make a difference. You see, in the recruiting world we are trained to say no. A lot. Like 99 per cent of the time. But what if my no came with encouragement. What if 'no you didn't get the job' came with coaching on how to nail it next time. No handouts, no free meal tickets. Just encouragement and a pathway to yes. A pathway to the American dream.

Yes, you can be the first in your family to achieve.

The honest truth is that I just fell in love with the opportunity youth of America. I fell in love with the promise they have. I fell in love with the 17-year-old Hispanic kid I met in Phoenix named Oscar that faces so many barriers in life. Income class, racial discrimination, violent surroundings, oh and he was deaf. I fell in love with the fact that he was willing to try. To put himself out there for the chance of hearing no once again. But today I witnessed humanity at is best. A store manager that has a history of working with the deaf interviewed him and hired him on the spot! He said YES!! And that was it for me. Interview after interview I watched kids get told YES. They were over the moon like it was nothing they had been told before. I LOVE them. I love the store managers that had to break to just cry because they were so overwhelmed with the need and the opportunities and genuine joy of these kids. Truly life-changing for everyone involved. I know it has changed me forever.

So here is my plea for anyone who reads this post. Fall in love. Fall in love with the youth of America. With Humanity. Fall in love with the American dream. Then tell someone something positive. Give encouragement and hope. Choose to follow your heart and not be a bystander. Do what I did... just be open to fall in love. I think you will.

What John was able to foster at Starbucks was jumping on a unique opportunity to identify the hidden genius in a whole population under-served and under-represented. He was part of a small team that started a movement, and he created a legacy that will touch the lives of individuals and communities for years to come. John is now replicating similar success at Amazon as he heads up Global Workforce Staffing, hiring hundreds of thousands of Amazonians around the world.

What cause do you care about and how can you extend it beyond the impact of your own company? 'Opportunity 100,000' was an initiative to tap into the genius in disadvantaged youth. Understanding the brilliance of teenage minds will help you identify how to lead those who are not like you.

Teenagers breaking rules and unlocking creative genius

We can learn a lot from teenagers, particularly how they act as though they are infallible and are always pushing what is possible. Brother and sister co-founders Shirah and Michael Bernade decided to create a solution to the drink-spiking epidemic. Shirah was going off to college and was increasingly scared of the stories her older friends told her of the dangers of going out and getting your drink spiked. One evening she took a hair scrunchie and some hosiery and designed the NightCap protector for drinks; it doubles as a hair tie.

I was delighted to learn neither Shirah or Michael had taken a business studies or entrepreneurial course at school, nor had studied it privately; instead they had seen an issue, wanted to solve the problem, and jumped in with two feet. They were already fundraising on crowdfunding site Indiegogo to take the product to market.

Here are four pieces of wisdom from the two teenage entrepreneurs:

- **Solving supply-chain challenges is the most crucial step for a product company.** 'The hardest part has been figuring out the entire supply chain for this product. As someone with no experience in the industry, I've had to understand all of the moving parts. The company that makes the fabric, the company that makes the elastic, the factory that makes the logo, the factory that puts together all of these things to create the product, the packaging company, the distribution company. How do they all work together? There is far more that goes into a product than I had originally thought and it makes me appreciate how other products are created.'
- **Make the most of your free resources at college.** If you have a great idea that you believe in, try to at least get it started when you're in college. You can get so many valuable resources that you will have to pay for out of pocket once you graduate.
- **Industry connections beat taking classes.** 'We've never taken a business class, an entrepreneurship class, or even a marketing class. All you need is the drive and passion to do something, the ability to think critically and solve problems, and be willing to reach out to people in the industry that can point you in the right direction, even if you don't know them.'
- **There are so many willing helpers.** 'As a young entrepreneur, the most important thing I did was surround myself with people who could fill in my knowledge gaps of an industry I knew little about. There are so many things you may not know, but especially being a young entrepreneur, there are almost always people who are willing to help and push you forward.'

Bringing the voice of youth into your company is an indicator of an innovative company that can create rapid growth in the right way. Consider how you can build connection and hear youthful voices in how you design, develop and deliver your products to your customers. You might just unlock some unknown hidden genius. Next we will explore how to lead marketing genius.

Managing your marketing genius

More than any other team member, your marketing genius will need help with translation, especially in explaining how their work translates to business results and impact. When John Schneider worked as VP of product marketing for software communications company Jive, he was able to use a filter for managing his marketing genius that can be applied to any company. Here is what he shared with me:

> My belief is that marketing really only has one goal and that is to make more sales for the business. As a marketing executive, I insist that it is my responsibility to define the revenue-generating initiatives that receive full go-to-market support, which makes me an accountable executive for pipeline, revenue and retention. This ensures my scope of my team's responsibility goes beyond more common activities like campaign management to include more strategic activities such as the evaluation of new market opportunities, expression of our vision in the market and the marketing plays that drive demand in the market.

> To illustrate, when I joined Jive we lacked focus surrounding our go-to-market strategy. We served dozens of buyer personas, more than any marketing organization could cater to effectively. We lacked an understanding of what happened to leads as they moved through the funnel. And our product roadmap lacked insight into what drove value for our customers.

> Through a data-driven prioritization effort and partnership with other key executives, I was able to focus the business on just three buyer personas, revise the addressable market data that indicated who buys our product, and define a new whole product strategy that was based on research that gave us definitive insights into the

purchase drivers of our product. The results spoke for themselves after this two-year transformation was completed, with pipeline growing beyond 4x coverage, the number of deals over $100K growing by 78 per cent, and discounting dropping by 38 per cent.

Sometimes your genius needs more than translation; timing, too, is essential, otherwise you will get rapid growth done wrong. Here's how one CEO was able to sense just when the time was right to unleash her own genius on the industry.

Jennifer Hyman founded clothing-rental company Rent the Runway when she looked inside her sister's jam-packed closet while her sister explained that she had nothing to wear. I heard Hyman speak at the Women of the Channel East Summit in New York in 2019. Hyman shared that her idea of everyone having a closet in the cloud where you could virtually pull from a collection was a leap too far for the fashion industry to understand or accept in 2009. Instead she started Rent the Runway on the premise of renting a dress for a special occasion. It was easier to understand the concept of hiring a cocktail dress just like a man hires a tuxedo. Sometimes you have to hold back your own genius until the world is ready to absorb it.

Sometimes your genius needs more than translation; timing, too, is essential, otherwise you will get rapid growth done wrong.

A decade later Hyman and her co-founder Jennifer Fleiss closed a $125 million round of investments led by Franklin Templeton Investments and Bain Capital Ventures; this valued the company at $1 billion.[1] This increased funding allowed expansion into children's clothing, homewares and warehousing expansion, but it has not all been a smooth ride. I have been a customer for 12 months and in addition to following reports of its financial success, I have seen how the company has emerged and how Hyman and her team have tackled their Rapid Growth Growing Pains.

Rapid Growth growing pains

As Rent the Runway expanded, introducing kids' clothes and homewares, mistakes started to happen, deliveries were delayed, unfulfilled or made in error. What I admired about the genius that Hyman and her team demonstrated was how candid they were, using the latest mechanisms for conversing with customers. It wasn't long ago when customer complaints were handled by telephone or in writing; now, with the immediacy of social media, your errors are no longer confined to private emails and phone calls – within seconds they can be broadcast to thousands or millions of listeners, customers, investors and the world.

During the implementation of a new warehouse system in 2019, Rent the Runway experienced a peak in issues. They have a dedicated Twitter account for support (@rtrhelp), and it provided a 24-hour response to issues from their customers who were noting that customer-service-phone-line response times could be up to two hours. Hyman also sent an email to all of their customers, clearly owning the issue, preparing for more disruption to come, and to ask for patience and understanding. This proactive communication from the heart goes a long way towards building connection with your customers.

Here's the email:

> We are committed to always being transparent and giving you the real play-by-play as we grow our business together. Over the last week and into the next few weeks, we are implementing significant changes to our operation. These changes will greatly improve your experience by increasing the selection you will have from our Unlimited closet. However, in the short term as we implement these changes, we know some of you are experiencing delays in shipments and therefore longer response times from our customer service team. Please know that the changes we are making will very quickly lead to more availability of the items you want and the consistent quality of customer experience you deserve.

We are working around the clock (myself included!) to implement these operational transformations as quickly as possible. Upgrading systems while still running the business at full speed is complex. We know that we will make some mistakes, so for the next month, if you have time-sensitive events, please order a few days earlier than you normally would. We are sorry, and we own this. Everything we are doing today is to improve your Rent the Runway membership for the long term and you should feel this improvement within the next three weeks.

We are beyond grateful for your commitment to Rent the Runway.

With gratitude,

Jenn Hyman

CEO and Co-Founder

I've been a customer of Rent the Runway for the past 12 months as I love the variety of clothes available and having the ability to wear an outfit when speaking on stage one week and then find a new one for my next event. I was recently due to leave for a family vacation in Orlando and then travel directly to an executive retreat in Newport Beach. My Rent the Runway closet delivery was due on the Monday of my flight, but only two of the five items arrived. I contacted the Rent the Runway Twitter help account and within hours they had set up delivery of my missing items to be sent straight to my hotel in Newport Beach. Soon after this, Rent the Runway announced a partnership with Marriot Hotels to set up Rent the Runway closets in select W Hotels. As reported in *New York Business Journal*, four locations will be launched in 2019: W Aspen, W Washington DC, W Hollywood and W South Beach.[2] It makes perfect sense to rent ski outfits, especially somewhere as fashion-focused as high-end ski resort Aspen. Hyman's genius continues to shine. What started as a service for renting only cocktail dresses has now expanded into skiwear, beachwear and even gym clothes, and is getting closer to her original vision of having a virtual closet in the cloud that delivers the clothes you need where you need them at the precise time you want to wear them. It shows what is possible when you know just how to manage your own genius and that of your teams.

In previous chapters we have explored various influence, communication and leadership techniques that create rapid growth. Next, we will uncover the critical role that pulls all of these growth paths together, the one that provides the seamless connections and insights across creative, technical and business teams – the role of the chief executive officer.

CHAPTER 8 RAPID RECAP

1 Pay your genius for their genius and then they won't become terrible people managers.

2 Know how to define who you are as a company so that every genius and everyone else feel connected, inspired and included.

3 You need to break rules when working with creative leaders and teams.

4 How can you challenge your company norms?

5 How can you free up your genius to do what they do best?

6 Help your marketing genius translate their genius into business impact.

7 Your enthusiasm and energy are contagious either way, so be deliberate.

8 How can you build connection and hear youthful voices in how you design, develop and deliver your products to your customers?

9 Test how ready the world is for your genius and that of your teams.

10 Be direct when you feel rapid growth growing pains.

Endnotes

1 Dickey, Megan Rose (March, 2019) Rent the Runway hits a $1 billion valuation, *TechCrunch*, https://techcrunch.com/2019/03/21/rent-the-runway-hits-a-1-billion-valuation (archived at https://perma.cc/VRS5-X9VC)
2 Noto, Anthony (December, 2019) Rent the Runway partners with Marriott for travel-wardrobe service, *New York Business Journal,* https://www.bizjournals.com/newyork/news/2019/12/05/rent-the-runway-partners-with-marriott-for-travel.html (archived at https://perma.cc/4P5K-L4JR)

CHAPTER NINE

The crucial role of the CEO for Rapid Growth

As we draw the ideas in this book to a close, there is one pivotal role that we need to return to, which was explored in Chapter 4 as we discussed succession planning. It is one of the least understood and most often misrepresented roles: that of a CEO. This chapter explores the most common myths and sets the record straight with the realities. These insights come from CEOs from my private CEO community, clients and those whose results set them apart as role models. If you are a CEO on your journey, you can learn from your peers, or if you work for a CEO or are curious about what to expect, you can understand and build some empathy for the leader holding that seat in your company.

The myths and realities of being a CEO

Myth 1: You have to know everything

Reality: Don't pretend to have all the answers.

Matt Carpenter, CEO of Silvercar, an Audi company, agreed:

The most obvious and unfair expectation of the CEO is expecting us to know everything. Similarly, the most obvious unreasonable behavior of a CEO is pretending we know everything. As a CEO, my primary responsibility is to make sure that the whole team knows that I do not have all the answers nor am I going to pretend that I have all the answers. Silvercar is a uniquely diverse organization in the sense that we manage very different businesses in very different environments. We run a B2C rental car business as well as a B2B enterprise software business. In our Austin office, about half of the team is technically driven – software engineers and product designers, who possess engineering, math and science backgrounds – and the other half is business-operations-driven sales and marketing professionals with more creative agility and higher risk tolerance. In this diverse and fascinating environment there isn't a single person who can be completely knowledgeable about everything related to our business and everything related to the enabling technology of our business.

Myth 2: You need a new North Star to make your mark

Reality: A new strategy is the easy part; executing against it will set you apart.

There is a reason strategy retreats are frequently happening in boardrooms and executives' offsites around the world. It is because they are the inspiring, fun part – exploring what is possible. The true work happens after the picture has been painted, or once a goal has been set.

Matt, the Silvercar CEO, agrees:

> I have to on a daily basis convince people that we have kind of a North Star and a mission and a core set of enabling behaviors that are super-critical to short-term and long-term success, but it is not just going to be me that communicates and portrays what all this is over time. My role is to give clarity and lead the team with an efficient decision-making process, but this is kind of a shared effort where we all have to be domain experts together, not rely on

the individual CEO. When feedback suggests some of my personal communications are too vague or nondescript, my leadership team is empowered to address their individual teams. If further clarification is necessary from me, topics can be put back on the table to address. We have no sacred cows at Silvercar, especially when it comes to communication.

Myth 3: CEOs have to call the important decisions

Reality: It is OK to rely on technology expertise from others to inform your decisions.

It is important to see how your technical, business and creatively minded teams influence and inform decisions. Matt from Silvercar had this interesting take on giving direction to engineering teams:

> Often technically inclined professionals, particularly engineers, are too accustomed to business leaders pretending they know everything and viewing engineering groups as simple service providers. So I think they've built up this scar tissue and they have this muscle memory where CEOs, primarily those with more business than technical experience, go into a room and make big, broad announcements without having the technical chops to know how all the magic actually happens (I think this scar tissue comes from not necessarily just our company, but experienced before their time at Silvercar). I've been more vulnerable, more open, more receptive to uncertainty and demonstrated a sincere and authentic intention to learn, particularly on the technical side of our business. That has worked out well.

Myth No. 4: The board meetings are crucial

Reality: Everything is influenced and decided before the board meeting.

While board meetings are an essential mechanism for running the business, the real work happens before and after the actual gathering of the board. Here is Matt's advice:

Don't surprise people in a meeting with a big pronouncement or a declaration. Don't put people on the spot or make them feel uncomfortable. It's so easy to build a coalition when you take the time to invest in one-on-one connections. I'm a big believer in this, especially if you're going to have data and facts that are going to defy their belief system or their norms.

Myth 5: Your questions need to be good enough to get it the first time

Reality: It is OK to keep asking until you truly understand.

I observed Jeff Bezos demonstrate this perfectly during my corporate days at Amazon; he was never afraid to admit when he didn't understand a finance projection, a technical explanation or just why we needed to sponsor the Met Gala to get Amazon into the forefront of fashion when we were launching designer fashion. He set the tone for what it was acceptable to be vulnerable about and encouraged the questioning of anything you didn't fully understand. Matt Carpenter follows the Bezos approach:

> Asking questions is so difficult for many leaders, especially CEOs. It is such an under-indexed skillset, the ability to be brave enough and inquisitive enough to ask for clarity when you don't understand something. Unfortunately, a lot of CEOs view it as a signal of weakness, worrying that they will be perceived as not sharp enough, not quick enough, not a good enough listener, but at the heart of it they just aren't brave enough and confident enough to ask questions.

Myth 6: If you have a big job, your partner needs to be at home

Reality: There is no one combination for success.

Despite all the advances in recent years, with CEOs there is still a common belief that you haven't succeeded unless you are the only one in your relationship working. Having the flexibility of a dual-career couple can work just as well, if not better, for some couples, as Matt described:

My wife and I decided a long time ago to make sure both of us had a chance to have really fulfilling, successful careers and we both do. My risk profile is underwritten by my partner managing a vibrant career on her own. My wife's career is equally important to mine. If something happens with mine, we still have hers and vice versa. I consider that a real partnership – not just in the spirit of risk management – but for us both to be the best versions of ourselves, which means that we have to act on our instincts and our judgment and everything else. We have to be us. It's easier to be us when we don't have all these kinds of dependencies, financial or social. Why bet on one pony when you can bet on two if it means that both ponies are better! This is not just for financial reasons, but just because I think it is the right way to steer and manage a partnership together.

My wife's career is just as important as mine.

Myth 7: If you have been a successful CEO once, you can immediately do it again

Reality: There are other factors that more closely correlate with the probability of success.

Meredith Amdur was able to increase the stock price of Wanted Analytics by 37 per cent in the first three months of her appointment, but does that mean she can automatically do it again at her next role? Possibly, but as she explained, there are greater factors that influence that success than the individual CEO:

When I took the CEO role at Wanted Analytics, it was in a tricky situation when I joined because it wasn't growing sufficiently. It was static. In some ways I had an easier journey. I had to reignite growth and I had the Board's support and I had the funding to do it. Those last two factors are not given in every CEO opportunity. I could claim to be a genius, but the reality was I had the right environment ready for me to use my strategic ability to make the right calls, fire up a team and position the team for significant fast stock growth and eventually sell the company at a premium.

Myth 8: Delivering results is the number one priority for any CEO

Reality: While results are crucial, building relationships and the confidence of the board and investors is the long-term play every CEO has to focus on.

Meredith was ahead of the game here, as she had served on Wanted's board for the previous 18 months. During that time she had been able to build deep relationships with the board chair and her board peers, so her entry as a CEO was able to build on these relationships. This enabled her to get insights and advice more rapidly than an outsider would have.

Myth 9: Once a CEO, always a CEO

Reality: Great experience accelerator as a tour of duty before then taking a chief marketing, chief strategy or chief technology role.

Meredith, who has worked for corporate giants, including Microsoft and Direct TV, and is now at her second CEO role, has a great perspective here:

> The experience of being a CEO in a smaller company perfectly positions you to return to mid-sized or larger companies and be an executive with a completely new lens. My next role could well be leading strategy for a division of a large company or running a division or a product group in a mid-sized to large company. My ego doesn't require me to be a CEO again, but I know my CEO and board experience have given me a unique perspective and ability to add value to a company in a variety of roles. I also know chief technology officers who are desperate to become CEOs, and

it would be the worst permanent move for them, as they would be moving away from the very area of expertise that makes them valuable, but as a two-year rotation in a company that needed that deep technical expertise at the top, it could be a great experience. Now that I have lived the CEO life, I have a different view on chief strategy officers, like the role I used to have at Direct TV and Microsoft. I would now insist they need to have experience managing a P&L; a prior CEO would be perfect because until your neck is on the line for executing the strategy, you can't truly understand. That is experience that no beautiful strategy PowerPoint can compensate for.

Myth 10: You can apply the same leadership approach and deliver success anywhere

Reality: You have to truly understand what is available to you and how to fund future growth in parallel.

A CEO in the retail industry discovered this when they accepted a role on the understanding that the product was far more evolved than they soon discovered was the case:

> I fast discovered that I had to fix the technology first. We had to rebuild the product, which meant putting an entirely new team in place. We needed the technology to differentiate us more dramatically in the market. This was holding us back from raising new funding, so we got stuck in a vicious cycle that stunted our turnaround.

Myth 11: It's about me

Reality: You need to be the authentic storyteller that helps your company shine.

Steven Webster, CEO of asensei, a technology company creating sportswear that tracks your progress and gives you real-time coaching feedback, lives in the much coveted, often misunderstood land of Silicon Valley. His experience in corporate giants like Adobe and Microsoft, combined with start-up experience, offers a blend of advice that any CEO can learn from – starting with what the public role and persona of a CEO needs to be. Here is what Webster shared:

> We live in the cult of celebrity, the cult of personality, the cult of the 'wantrepreneur.' Living in the Bay Area, there's an entire community of wantrepreneurs. When someone asks me what I do, I don't reply 'I'm an entrepreneur.' I reply that 'I work in sports technology.' If pressed, I'll tell you a little bit about the product: 'We solve the problem of how to coach sport at digital scale.'
>
> Push me some more and I'll reveal a little bit about the solution: 'We've developed technology for smart sports apparel, and a platform for sports coaching.' Then if pressed further with 'What do you do there?' I'll reply, 'Actually, I started the company four or five years back.' I identify with the problem, I identify with the solution, I identify with the customer, I identify with the team, all before I identify with 'I'm the founder' or 'I'm the CEO.'
>
> Brad Feld, one of the most thoughtful VCs in the industry, recently shared a perspective that I like. It was about the nuanced difference between thought-leadership and personal brand building: When I stand on stage and keynote at an event such as the Consumer Electronics Show, as confident as people think I might look up there, I'm banking on them listening to what I'm saying about the category and the company, not judging or forming opinion about me. I think one of the biggest myths in the world of the start-up CEO is the myth that you have to be this visionary, enigmatic founder. The Elon Musk. The Steve Jobs. The Richard Branson.

We live in the cult of celebrity, the cult of personality, the cult of the 'wantrepreneur.'

Rather, you need to be an authentic storyteller. You need to be able to clearly articulate the vision – to your team, to investors, to customers, to partners. But the idea that you have to be the protagonist in your company story, and that the identity of the company is tied to the identity of the founder? I think it's the exception, not the norm.

Myth 12: You work for yourself as a start-up CEO

Reality: You are the one working for all of those involved.

There is much delusion around the role of start-up CEOs. Many large company corporate executives crave the illusion of freedom that they anticipate a start-up provides, but few make the transition as successfully as asensei CEO Steven Webster. He explained to me how the illusion of working for yourself just is not a reality:

As soon as you take investment, you work for your investors. As soon as you take institutional investment, you work for your board and for your shareholders. If you are in any way successful in raising capital for your venture, any Invictus-inspired notion of being the 'master of your fate, captain of your soul' will quickly evaporate.

Before you have taken money from someone else, if you've found an authentic voice with which you can tell a story about a future that doesn't exist yet, and have recruited Argonauts on your quest, then you're also not working for yourself. I'm inspired by the ideas of servant leadership; that as a leader or CEO your role is to serve those around you, not for them to serve you. This is especially true in an early-stage company, which can feel like a crazy quest, at the end of which there might be a Golden Fleece, provided we don't drown at sea in a storm first, get turned into stone by a woman with snakes for hair or get killed by re-animated skeletons from the dead. I truly

As soon as you take investment, you work for your investors.

believe the CEO needs to acknowledge that they wake up every day working for the people who have joined them on this perilous journey.

So, the reality is that the CEO is working for a broad set of stakeholders, with all the pressure and responsibilities to show up and measure up. You're working for your customers, your partners, your board, your investors, your team that you hired. You're working for your family, who encouraged you, pushed you even, to take the leap, but now you realize how hard they're working, for longer than they signed up for, and for a quality of life that's an investment in 'what if', not 'what was'.

It's a myth indeed that you're working for yourself, unless you're working alone. For sure, you don't serve one master. You traded that to serve many.

Myth 13: Everyone else is 'crushing it'

Reality: Overnight success takes years of preparation.

The success calibration can knock you off course, especially if you don't surround yourself with those in similar roles, at similar altitudes in a company. Webster shares just how important that is to break the ill-informed belief that everyone else is succeeding while you are floundering:

> I'm lucky to have a tight network of former colleagues and friends, all of whom, within the same period of time, went on to start companies and grow in the CEO role. It's a support network of people who all know about the difficulties of fundraising, hiring, the board meeting that went south, the product launch that slowly lifted toward the sky but hasn't punched through the atmosphere just yet. Ask any of us, and I'll hazard that a majority know the imposter syndrome of being the CEO of a temporary organization in search of a business model.

Spend your time on VC Twitter, read the tech press, and you're only exposed to the outliers. The team that raised $50 million for their pre-revenue pre-launch product that's got to displace PowerPoint to succeed. The founder that ran a fundraising process in two weeks by telling everyone that if they didn't meet them by next Friday, they'd miss out. The product launch that had 1 million users within three months, and 50 per cent month on month viral growth.

The rest of us aren't crushing it like that. People I know that are exceptional individuals don't get these exceptional results either. I can't tell you how many times I've watched the locker room speech by Al Pacino in the movie *Every Given Sunday*. The inches we need are all around us. In every break of the game. And we fight for each inch. We tear ourselves and everyone around us for those inches. Because we know that winning is about adding up those inches. It's a game of inches. And you win by surrounding yourself with people who will fight for those inches with you.

This is the most dangerous of myths – the entrepreneur who is crushing it, the abundance of capital and the ease of getting it, that if you're not holding three term sheets in your first week of fundraising or have the #1 spot in the AppStore, it's a signal that maybe you're failing. Those myths are dangerous, as they don't just attack the founder's head, they start to attack the body.

You're not crushing it. Because most overnight successes take years of preparation.

Myth 14: Global businesses can all be run the same way

Reality: There are crucial rules to follow if you want success globally.

This final myth-buster comes from a roundup of all my global experiences in my corporate life combined with my speaking and workshops around the world. I have distilled the reality into five crucial Global Rules every CEO needs to oversee:

1 **Check that your well-intended team activities will work**
'Eye of the Tiger' starts playing. A very excited, whooping CEO comes running down the aisles screaming at the top of his voice 'I LOVE THIS COMPANY!' I'll never forget my first company all-hands at Microsoft with Steve Ballmer running in to greet the 25,000 employees packed into Safeco field baseball stadium. Most of the US-based crowd loved it. But had he tried that in front of a European audience, he would not have had the same wave-your-hands-in-the-air-and-cheer reaction. Don't assume that everyone on a global team will want to participate in what is normal for your home country. Check first. (From this European, please stop forcing people to dance at the start of events. 'YMCA' might be fun for some, but not everyone wants to do that.)

2 **Your company culture beats country norms**
The HQ country often sets the company tone for how decisions are taken, communication occurs and promotions and rewards are made. Learn that fast and don't assume country stereotypes are always true.

3 **Figure out your time zones fast**
I can't believe I am writing this basic one, but you would be surprised at how many non-urgent calls get scheduled for 9 pm on a Friday night. Time & Date has a brilliant meeting planner and can add your global cities on your iPhone to your world clock, so you always know what time it is when you call, text or IM.

4 **Understand how brilliant you need to be at sharing your brilliance**
How acceptable is it for you, and how comfortable are you talking about your achievements? Historically, this is harder for Europeans than it is for their US colleagues. But your company culture dictates what is acceptable and expected. Find out fast so you don't suffer like I did when I moved from

the UK to Seattle with Xbox and was shocked in my performance review when I was told I was average. That happened because I wasn't brilliant at shining a spotlight on my brilliance. It just wasn't how I was brought up and I was worried about being braggadocio.

5 **Hire globally if you manage globally**
How many of your team were born elsewhere? Lived in other countries? Can speak languages that you need in your global business? You can't run a global business with a group of locals, so make sure your company reflects your global market.

CHAPTER 9 RAPID RECAP

1 Be OK with not having all the answers.

2 Success in execution beats success in strategy.

3 You don't always have to call the shots.

4 Know the power outside of board meetings.

5 Ask endless questions.

6 Your partner being at home is not a badge of success for everyone.

7 A CEO doesn't always have to be a CEO.

8 Overnight success takes years of preparation.

9 Corporate executives transitioning to start-up CEO requires a unique skill.

10 Understand the global rules for success.

Now that you have discovered the top myths and realities of CEOs who create rapid growth, whether you are a CEO, aspire to be or work for one, reflect on how you can apply the lessons of these myth-busters to your own team. Chapter 10 will explore what happens if you don't and your rapid growth goes wrong.

CHAPTER TEN

Rapid Growth Done Wrong: what you can learn from getting fired

There is a secret that is seldom openly discussed in rapidly growing companies. It happens far more than you realize, and you learn phenomenal lessons when it happens to you. But because it is never talked about, others don't have the opportunity to learn from the lessons – until now, that is. In this chapter you will learn how to deal with the unexpected, unwanted, but often priceless lessons from not getting what you want exactly when you want it. You will learn lessons from getting fired or pushed out. You will hear the harsh stories and hindsight lessons from those who have experienced rapid growth, and what happens when it has gone wrong, resulting in significant impact to the company or to personal careers. Several executives contributed stories to this chapter; you will hear their voices but they won't be identified. I am thankful to each one of them for sharing their insights with me, and each of them said how helpful it was to stop, deconstruct and extract lessons from the time they were fired or pushed out. I am delighted to be able to be the vehicle for sharing those lessons with you all.

The unspoken topic of failure

We don't talk about failure enough, not in companies, not in schools, not on sports teams, not anywhere – and it is affecting how we prepare future generations for accepting that outcomes may not always be positive. I was mortified to find out that wealthy parents used their money to protect their kids from experiencing failure in the shocking US college application scam. Over 50 families had evidence brought against them alleging that they had paid to have someone pave the way for their child to enter their college of choice.

As parents, we teach our daughters the Three Golden Rules of Failure that every leader needs to teach their teams about failure:

• You won't always win.
• You won't always get what you want.
• The door you want to open won't always open exactly when you want it to.

When we are growing in life or in our careers, we learn the most from our disappointments. Here are three of my most gutting experiences that didn't end so badly after all:

• I remember being absolutely gutted that Cadbury didn't hire me on their management training scheme because I failed their entry test. But I went on to join House of Fraser's management training scheme, which supported my business

196

and finance degree at night school, and I went on to lead a team of 25 at the age of 21.

- I was mortified when consulting firm Arthur Anderson wouldn't hire me because I had a part-time degree and didn't attend university full-time. But I then joined Marconi and got to travel to Milan, Munich and Dublin on the corporate jet as part of my global role before I was 30.
- I was heartbroken that we reduced the scope of the outsourcing deal between Marconi and CEC at the 11th hour so that my department was no longer part of the transfer, but then I joined Xbox, which led to them relocating me to Seattle and I got to be part of the team that created the *Guinness Book of World Records*–winning Kinect Camera.

I work with extremely successful executives, many of whom have experienced not getting their perfect job the first time, have occasionally been fired, or have screwed up a product launch. I tell them each the same thing: you will learn more from your mistakes than from your successes. When one door doesn't open, it can be surprising what comes next. If we can't teach others how to survive disappointment, how will they survive without us cushioning every fall when we move onto our next opportunity?

It is not just kids who need to toughen up. Help your teams today to get a thicker skin without second-guessing and protecting every possible mistake or inadequacy. You can start by learning from these executive failures and consider how you can share your own examples with those around you.

The harsh reality of getting pushed out or fired

This is something you will be reluctant to talk about when it is about to happen, during the time it is happening or shortly after it has happened. But when you are actually going through it is precisely the moment you need to get advice about it.

I have observed how executives disappear from view. They avoid conferences, events, being present on social media and returning colleagues' messages, because it is a hard spot to be in. As soon as you lose the brand or company associated with your job title, you are often uninvited to executive community events because you are no longer part of a corporate invite or sponsorship arrangement.

Getting fired or pushed out is nothing to be ashamed of or embarrassed by, and it happens far more than many people realize, but because no one talks about it and everyone covers it up and puts on smiles and pithy reactions because of legal documents signed, all those insightful lessons are lost.

At many companies when you leave suddenly, there is judgment. People assume you failed, assume you were fired. Wrong assumptions are made about you not delivering, or knowing how to work the internal relationships, and it is easier to get a job when you have a job precisely because of these biases and judgments. This is because many only hear the corporate narrative and not the real story of what happened behind the scenes. People don't talk, not simply because it is unprofessional, but also because it is likely they are under some sort of a severance-package agreement and mutual non-disparagement arrangement. So nobody learns from what is truly happening.

Getting fired or pushed out is nothing to be ashamed of or embarrassed by.

The more you create rapid growth and rise in altitude throughout your career, the more likely it is going to happen to you. Brace yourself. As I was writing this book, executives were encouraging me to include this topic, as it has never been written about before. It occurred to me that while this topic could be a book in and of itself, I had to shine a spotlight on this never-talked-about phenomenon because rapid growth companies, products and innovations are high-risk, high-reward scenarios. If you aren't getting fired, you are not being bold enough or pushing the boundaries of possibilities. Trust me: at some point your rapid-growth career will result in you getting fired or pushed out.

The names have been hidden to protect the individuals' stories, but the lessons are all still here. Let's start with the different stages you will experience.

Five stages of getting fired or pushed out

1 **Obliviously satisfied**
   - You have no clue what is about to happen.
   - You could have a phase of phenomenal success that may be long- or short-lived.
2 **Doubts start to form**
   - Your boss has had a moment, a trigger, an incident, and doubt is now forming about your future.
   - It could be minor or major, but the warning signs now might start to show.
   - Your boss, board or investors could have changed, which then sows the seeds of doubt.
   - This stage could be skipped completely.
3 **The explosive incident**
   - Your boss could be fired.
   - There could be a takeover.
   - Business results could be unexpectedly disappointing.
   - A perceived or real conduct issue could have occurred.
4 **Cheerio!**
   - The exit could be a slow, drawn-out, looming ending.
   - The exit might happen in hours, not days or weeks.
   - Sometimes you could be walked out within hours.
   - There could be a moment of debate if demotion, change of role or a sharp exit occurs.
5 **The Aftermath**
   - Who stepped into your shoes?
   - The message will vary.

- Your credibility may be impacted.
- It may be a complete mystery to you and others.
- You likely can't control the communication.
- You possibly have to sign away your right to talk about it or talk negatively about the company or leaders involved.
- Prepare for your individual reverberations.

As you read this chapter, you may relate to the examples provided, or you may feel compelled to share your story and lessons. You can anonymously send it to me by visiting www.whenigotfired. com, because then others could benefit from your wisdom just like you have here.

'When I got fired', executive examples

Example one: too fast, too disruptive

The situation

As a new president of a billion-plus company within a multibillion-dollar organization, I was promoted internally based on achievements in a different part of the enterprise and moved to a part of the enterprise that was struggling to address performance issues.

I placed my focus on delivering results and having been placed as a 'change agent', I set to work identifying opportunities and changes in process strategy and team skill set that needed addressing.

Eighteen months into my tenure and in spite of improving and delivering strong financial performance, I was rapidly exited from the business.

Early warning signs

I replaced the new CEO, and although he said he wanted my disruptive changes, the reality was different when I started changing the very processes and team that he had put in place.

I noticed a surprising reluctance to let me act on the observations that I was making about the executive team changes that we needed to make in order to deliver the speed and scale of change that I thought we had agreed to implement. I was having the brakes put on me everywhere I turned.

I had failed to spot the long-standing personal relationships that existed between my leadership team and my CEO, who had hired them all. To make matters worse, there was a social aspect to the relationships, and my leadership team would meet each other and my CEO at weekends. I wasn't invited. The ties were never cut. They continued to run their ideas by him rather than me. I was like a sheepdog in a field trying to shepherd the team in a new direction, but in fact they dug in and got even closer together, following the previous sheepdog. My bark had no bite.

I was like a sheepdog in a field trying to shepherd the team in a new direction.

How did it happen?

Veiled under a cost-cutting exercise – 'let's eliminate some executive costs' – I was told my position had been eliminated. In a rare moment of candor, my CEO told me that while I delivered results, I had tried to implement too many changes that threatened my team, peers and the CEO himself. They wanted a disruptor, and I delivered results, but they didn't truly want to disrupt to the point of making people-changes that impacted their friendship circles.

What blunt advice would you give yourself in hindsight?

- Evaluate and know what you are getting into by asking the right questions from the outset before accepting the role.
- Make empowerment a condition of acceptance; make sure that I can operate my own team.
- Evaluate and understand the unwritten rules of social connections and friendships.

- Find a way of assessing openness to change.
- Know how to moderate the pace of change according to acceptance or speed of adaptation from those around you.
- The situation was not operating as a professional culture but an odd mix of personal and friendship trust, not necessarily based on performance. I had not experienced this before.
- I didn't initiate setting the ground rules with my new boss.
- I didn't spot that even within the same organization there can be diverse cultural environments depending on the department.
- I did not see that the culture of many years of a team working together would feel threatened enough by having a new leader, let alone one who had new ideas and perspectives.
- I wasn't able to make my own hires in order to dilute the established group-think.
- I mistakenly took my appointment to the role as a sign of unwavering support from my CEO. I didn't test or verify this. I took it for granted.
- I made the profound mistake of underestimating personal relationships in the work environment. This may have been cultural.
- Looking back, I was set up to fail from the start. I only realize that now.

Example two: a test of my morals cost me my job

Situation

In my role as an executive I was asked if I wanted to participate in a scheme that was morally wrong. I declined and explained that I would have to inform our general counsel. What I didn't realize was this set up a chain reaction that would rapidly escalate and cost me my job.

Early warning signs
There were none. It was a complete surprise.

How did it happen

Within days I was asked to leave. The reason stated was cost-cutting, but I was informed informally that the CEO wasn't ready to expose (or stop) the current practices that would have exposed a large proportion of the executive team.

What blunt advice would you give yourself in hindsight?

- I wouldn't change a thing, but I did learn many lessons.
- I could never have anticipated it, I couldn't have uncovered it through due diligence prior to accepting the role, and I absolutely was confident it was the right action to take.
- Sometimes you can't predict the unexpected and cannot tell if it is a test of your moral boundaries and how much you are prepared to look the other way.
- I can sleep at night knowing I did the right thing, even if it cost me a blip in my career and I had to go through the painful process of finding a new role, which involved having to move to an obscure part of Europe.
- Sometimes you have to decide whether you're going to speak out and risk getting sidelined or fired. Or whether you are willing to shut up and be complicit.

Example three: when you join with the wrong job title

Situation

I really wanted to work for this global technology company. They wowed me throughout the hiring process, and gave me compensation and stock beyond my wildest dreams, but they refused to budge on the job title. It resulted in me getting hired as a senior director, not as VP, despite being an SVP and two levels below the CEO of a similar-sized company.

When it started to go wrong

From my first week, I noticed problems getting introduced to the right altitude leader as part of my launch into the company.

Despite my significant-sized organization and my gargantuan budget, I didn't have the right two letters to get the right invites to the right offsites, strategy previews and meetings. It cost me my job. I had to quit. I could not be successful and the hoops I had to jump through to get an internal promotion were too high and the timeframe was impossible.

What blunt advice would you give yourself in hindsight?

- Find out just how important job titles are for access, decisions, power and freedom in the company you are about to join.
- Get really candid about your budget control and freedom to decide and act.
- Be prepared to walk away if you are tethered at the wrong altitude and you will be held back.
- Job titles are like candy: you can give them out for next to nothing, but some types are just as attractive and addictive as sugar. If you don't have the right one, you are doomed from the start.
- Find out just how title-sensitive the company is if you don't get the title you think you deserve. It can also cause you to get pushed out if you don't have the right one just when you need it.

Example four: all my supporters left

Situation

I failed to proactively influence the right senior people, and all of my supporters left within six weeks. I became anonymous just at the time when I needed my executive supporters around me.

When it started to go wrong

I suspected my boss was going to get tapped to run a company, as she was passed over for the CEO role, and her experience meant she wasn't ready to be number two to one of her previous peers. I had three other supporters at the executive team and board level, so I wasn't concerned.

How did it happen?

Within four weeks of the new CEO taking over he had reorganized and changed 67 per cent of the leadership team. I could see the writing on the wall. I had to quickly build a relationship with my new boss, who joined from outside the company. He made a fast decision to bring in one of his previous team to replace me. I didn't have other supporters left on the executive team to fight for me to take a different role, so I was asked to leave.

What blunt advice would you give yourself in hindsight?

I failed to proactively influence the right senior people, and all of my supporters left within six weeks.

- I needed to have thought through five executive chess moves ahead. Had I done so, I would have predicted that this had a high probability of happening.
- I didn't work on my External Personal Stock Valuation, as I was heads down saving the company millions and delighting our customers with new services. I put the company and shareholders far too far ahead of my personal equitable rewards for the impact I was making.
- You cannot fix years of neglecting building the right relationships in a matter of days and weeks.
- I should have prioritized how to influence the right people as part of my regular day job, not waiting to do it when I needed it most.

Example five: when you have a wakeup call while on stage speaking at a conference

Situation

It took someone in the audience telling me I was full of rubbish to make me realize I had to fire myself.

When it started to go wrong

I planned to stay at the company two years maximum to turn around everything I could see was wrong that the company said they wanted to change. Five years later I was still there. This should have been my early warning system: that five years later I hadn't delivered what should have been delivered in 18 months.

How did it happen?

There was an event where I was the keynote speaker. During the question time a woman came up to the microphone and after thanking me for a great speech she told me that she had heard me speak five years ago and had gone back to her company and shared all the wisdom and they implemented my advice. Then she heard me speak two years ago, and she again went back to her company and shared my brilliance with her team. Today she told me how she had taken out her notebook to take copious notes about everything I was doing with my team. She then told me at 15 minutes into my talk she put down her pen and stopped taking notes. She was one of our customers and told me I was full of complete rubbish because the story I was telling on stage was not what she felt when she walked in our stores. It was at that precise moment I knew I had to fire myself, as I hadn't been able to make the progress I wanted to.

What blunt advice would you give yourself in hindsight?

- Media training works! I wanted to say you're exactly right. We are full of rubbish. This is all jargon. It's all rhetoric. The preparation I had for analyst calls paid off. I felt inauthentic. It is kind of all a lie because we're a big, dysfunctional mess internally. That's what I wanted to say. Of course, other words came out of my mouth that were company-appropriate, and the PR team would have been proud of me, but, in my heart, I knew it was all false. On the plane back to New York I just kept remembering her question.

- Taking time to stop and take a step back to evaluate what I was doing was valuable.
- Hold true to your original goal. I always told myself I would give it two years to try and if I couldn't effect change, I'd leave. Then all of a sudden, I was approaching five years in my role.
- Notice when the gravitational force of the traditional ways of operating are too strong for you alone.
- Test if you are really building up advocates within the business.
- Notice what detractors are in place and if you truly can overcome them.
- When the person who hires you leaves, check if you truly have the supporters to continue or ask yourself if you should quit too.
- Ask yourself whether you are fighting too hard to make changes in the business.
- Consider where you can take your passion, your approach and your tolerance for change, and apply it where it will be appreciated.

These five executive stories pull back the curtain and share the realities of working in fast-growing companies where you make bold bets. The rewards can be phenomenal, but so can the risks.

If you are having a bad day after getting fired, remember all the other successes you have delivered in your career. Consider the scale, impact, and success that you have achieved. Call one of your inner circle of advisors, or go back and read all the praise you have previously received. (You write that down and keep it in one spot, right? If not, it is time to start for times just like this one.)

The type of leader that succeeds and creates rapid growth gets fired and pushed out – and does it with style, grace and confidence. Hopefully, these examples start to lift the shroud of secrecy that surrounds getting fired and give you some hindsight advice that allows you to prepare for that inevitable day.

CHAPTER 10 RAPID RECAP

1 You learn far more from a terrible experience than a great one.

2 No CEO, board or boss is perfect, but you fast learn new questions to ask or due diligence to perform before you say yes to your next role after getting fired.

3 You need to have a confidential sounding board to tell you what to pay attention to and what is crazy and not your fault.

4 You need to create a Personal Force Field that protects your sense of self-worth so they don't steal your confidence, swagger and the very thing others will hire you for.

5 In your next role don't swing the pendulum the other way for whatever you were fired for.

6 You versus tenure = you often losing.

7 The dynamics of what goes on outside the meetings, board rooms and office time is far more powerful than inside.

8 Refusing to compromise your morals is a test worth passing even if you get fired.

9 You might know the illegal reason you were fired, but it will be hard to prove or might be covered up.

10 The HBO TV series *Succession* is closer to reality than any CEO or board would care to publicly admit. Watch it for insights and your amusement.

Having discovered the worst that can happen and prepared you for all eventualities when rapid growth can go wrong, let's look at how you can track and accelerate your success.

CHAPTER ELEVEN

How to track and accelerate your success

I t never ceases to amaze me how poorly companies set, monitor and manage goals at every level of the company. Sales teams don't know their sales targets until the end of the first quarter, specific targets aren't set for key strategic initiatives, or vague agreements of collaboration are made at senior levels and not implemented at every level of the company.

Most goal-setting processes are ineffective because they focus on a spreadsheet, a complex tool or a laborious process that discourages the very effectiveness you are trying to drive across your company. What you will find in this chapter are pragmatic tools you can implement with minimum technology and maximum impact, along with stories of what accelerates and decelerates the results you want to see. Let's examine first the start-of-the-year fallacy that distracts everyone.

Why resolutions don't work

Resolutions are what make gym businesses boom around the world each January. The annual flurry of new and old members actually showing up to work out fuels the revenue success throughout the whole year.

The January flurry also happens in businesses. Bosses everywhere try new approaches, promise to communicate better, take care of their employees, become more strategic, innovate more or perhaps build their external network. But they will only succeed if their new habits are embedded into their daily life, not just for January.

Instead of looking at your work resolutions, look at why you need to reset them in the first place. What mechanisms were not in place that caused you to get where you are? I am working with one of my new clients on a new product roadmap for their business, but in parallel we are also developing a system so that there will be no future surprises. It's called the Rapid Growth Rhythm (see Figure 11.1).

We all know what happens to a band when they don't have rhythm. Perhaps you've seen that at one of your child's concert performances? It feels disjointed and awkward, and the same happens when companies don't have rhythm. Your team gets out of step, you don't know what tune you are trying to play and the audience will cringe.

FIGURE 11.1 The Rapid Growth Rhythm

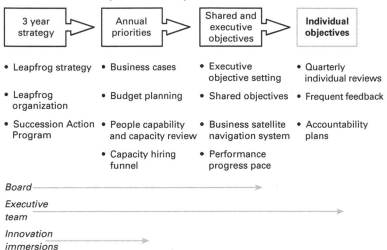

Want to see how in rhythm your business is? The Rapid Growth Rhythm guide will help you end the year without the need to set ANY resolutions in the next because you will already be performing at the top of your game. To perform your Rapid Growth Rhythm Review, ask your executive team these questions:

- Do we have a three-year Leapfrog Strategy in place? (Chapter 4)
- Have we determined our Leapfrog Organization to achieve our strategy? (Chapter 4)
- Do we have a CEO and Executive Team Succession Plan in place? (Chapter 4)
- Are we clear on our annual priorities?
- Do we have a robust budget-plan process and reality?
- Do we review our people capabilities and capacity to deliver?
- Have we calculated our Capacity Hiring Funnel? (Chapter 7)
- Has every leadership team shared objectives where relevant?
- Does every employee have individual objectives?
- Are objectives tracked and is feedback shared quarterly?

You need to have every single step complete if you truly want to create rapid growth. Now that you have made it this far in the book, you can go back to each of the chapters to find more specific support, but the most important part is knowing how to make sure your goals are clear in the first place.

Five steps to goal-setting that work

Here is a fast way to create goals that deliver rapid growth:

1 First, make sure you take your executive team goals and use those to inform your own goals and those of your team.
2 Ask your team to set individual goals for themselves and their team.
3 Ask your team to complete a list of initiatives, requests and goals that you will NOT achieve this year but that you can cascade upwards and sideways to reset expectations.
4 Put in place quarterly check-ins to review, edit and track progress of your goals and those of your teams.
5 Allow no surprises when it is compensation review time and people are expected to be rewarded for what they have delivered.

Sometimes it is easier to spot when it is not going to plan so you can course-correct along the way. Here's what happens when goal-setting fails.

Goal-setting gone wrong

Consider where you are right now in your fiscal year; maybe not everyone on your team has clear goals. In fact, you are still working on your own priorities and haven't yet agreed on them with your boss. I understand. Multiple priorities can distract you from articulating and communicating goals to your organization, but the lost productivity of a team adrift without a destination is far greater than some realize. I have been working with many of my executive clients on developing robust and meaningful goals rapidly. Here are the six biggest mistakes I see when executives are setting goals for their teams:

- **You fail to mention profit, revenue, costs, market share and business-impacting metrics.** Recently, I was working with a newly appointed technology executive whose organization is viewed as detached from the business. We created meaningful goals that were framed in the language of what the business needs to achieve market share and revenue growth.

Put in place quarterly check-ins to review, edit and track progress of your goals.

- **You spend so long developing them that they are irrelevant when published.** A sales organization I worked with never gave their sales team their sales targets until 12 weeks into the new fiscal year as they waited for the goals to cascade from above. The calendar year is no surprise, so we reduced and shifted their planning cycle so that sales teams knew on day one of the fiscal year what was expected from them and were no longer adrift for 25 per cent of their year.

- **Your process, systems and technology for capturing goals is so arduous everyone avoids completing them.** All you need is a list that you can share. I have seen more complex performance management systems than JPL used to get rover on Mars.

- **You create goals in a silo.** Many executive teams create goals in a vacuum and treat them as trade secrets among their own executive peers. Look left and right across your technical, creative and business teams to make sure everyone's goals are heading in the same direction.

- **You ignore your people.** You forget to include a goal that is focused on building leaders and an organization that will accelerate your results (and no, that doesn't mean training!).

- **Your process becomes a source of company amusement.** If the forms, questions and information requested are so pointless that people start ridiculing them, that's trouble. I knew of one leader who told me every year he had written a comical paragraph in his goals to test whether anyone actually read them, and nobody ever did.

Ask yourself what impact your organization will have on your company profits, revenue and market share and hook your goals into those metrics. This is a crucial step in being a Trilingual Executive as outlined in Chapter 3.

Are we there yet?

'*Are we there yet?*' used to be a familiar cry from the back seat of our car when I was sitting with my sister and brother on family adventures driving around the British countryside. My dad loved surprises, everything was a surprise, and we never knew where we were going until we got there. Even if we guessed by following along with the paper maps in the back seat or reading the road signs, Dad would never give in and tell us our destination. This might sound familiar to some teams and their own leadership.

Now we have electronic navigation systems such as Google Maps and Waze that accurately predict the time to your destination and crowdsources real-time incident data to re-route you around roadblocks. Can you say the same for your current year's business goals? Now, on our family drives the 'Are we there yet?' has been replaced by 'How many minutes until we get there?', followed by 'but that's just gone up – you said 37 minutes, now it's 43?!'

The technology might have advanced from maps to apps for your car journeys, but do you truly know the real ETA for your product launches and initiatives this coming year?

YOUR BUSINESS SATELLITE NAVIGATION SYSTEM
Ask yourself these three critical questions to determine if your Business Satellite Navigation System is pointing to where it should be:

1 Does everyone have a shared understanding of the 'you are here' point of progress?
2 Are you satisfied with your months of progress given where you are in your financial year?
3 Do you have a re-route recovery plan if your planned time for reaching your destination is later than planned?

That way you can make sure that when your board asks 'Are we there yet?' you can confidently answer with precision. Once goals are clear and you know how you are progressing, it is time to focus on the resources you need to lead delivery of rapid growth. This is often left to the recruitment, staffing and human resources function – do that at your peril. While this isn't a fluffy soft-skills book, I do want to point out the critical nature of your owning your role in hiring a fully staffed team, because without it, you will exhaust your existing team and fail to unlock the actual impact that your products and services can have on your customers. You simply won't deliver fast enough.

How to get a fully staffed team for rapid growth

Imagine your life if you were at 100 per cent headcount with zero vacant positions to hire for. You would, of course, accelerate the rate and quality of what you deliver to the company. It might seem as far-fetched as winning the lottery, but it is closer than you think and just as valuable. The key is to avoid getting distracted with delivering and responding to your CEO/board/customer demands, which seem desperately important right now. But nothing is more of a priority than filling your vacant job positions. Here are five ways to rapidly do that:

- Make sure the ball is not in your court.
  Consider all of the job vacancies you are hiring for. Are others relying on you to send them information, make a decision or make progress? If so, it is time to return the serve and make sure that the ball isn't in your court to avoid preventable delays.

- Don't rely on your recruiters to recruit for you.
  Every recruiter I have ever met is ridiculously overloaded. Business leaders have unrealistic expectations about what their recruitment teams can actually do for them. You have to take ownership for hiring key roles yourself, or provide the right capacity and capability for your recruitment teams.
- Tell your network who you are looking to hire.
  I hold an invite-only executive-community event, bringing together CEOs and senior executives, called the Wright Exchange. An unexpected bonus of the event is the spontaneous referrals and recommendations that executives give each other for their job vacancies. Are you letting your network know who you want to hire?
- Spend 50 per cent of your time hiring.
  As unthinkable as this is, if you have a direct report opening on your team, you need to prioritize 50 percent of your time preparing, assessing and interviewing candidates for that position. You won't get fast traction without it.
- Temporarily over-invest in your hiring pipeline.
  One company I worked with was desperately under-resourced and their vacant job positions were severely impacting their ability to deliver their revenue goals. I showed them how their hiring pipeline couldn't even keep up with their usual attrition levels, never mind the new roles they wanted to hire. We calculated that the company had to invest seven figures to hit their hiring plan. They approved, we implemented it and they hit record profit levels that year because they had hit their hiring plan, showing a nine-times return on investment. Is your hiring pipeline dehydrated and costing you money?

Every recruiter I have ever met is ridiculously overloaded.

You make choices every day about where you spend your time and so does your team. How can you refocus today? You need to realize that it is OK to be unfair.

Be unfair

One critical way to improve how you accelerate your success is to be unfair. I was running a leadership retreat for Ingram Micro managers on innovation and leadership, and a question came from a leader in the room about how much time they had to spend on corrective coaching and performance management. They were frustrated and wishing they could spend more time with their high performers. When I explained they could prioritize their time to do just that, their eyes lit up with all of the possibilities that would be created: increased sales, improved market share, launching new events that would delight customers, all because they were unfairly allocating their time to their top performers.

Your job as a leader is not to be fair:

- Unfairly allocate your time among your team, spending more time with your newest and highest-performing people.
- Unfairly treat your promotion budget as a pot to be unevenly distributed, rewarding your most successful team members.
- Unfairly pick which meetings are graced with your presence. Don't feel you have to show because you were invited or haven't been for a while.

I regularly advise executives I work with of my 50 per cent rule. If you have open headcount on your immediate team, you need to spend 50 per cent of your time hiring for that role – defining, outreaching to your network, interviewing, validating and preparing for the new recruit's first year in that role. Nothing holds you back as an executive more than being one or two people down on your team. That might seem like an unfair balance of your time, but it is just what is needed.

Complaints about fairness come from kids for a reason. I have my own laboratory at home to prove this, with nine-year-old twin girls and their 11-year-old sister. Whether it is who got the most carrots on the dinner plate, who last sat next to which parent at the movie theatre, or whose turn it is to put the star on top of the Christmas tree, they are keeping a running tally of fairness points so they can cry foul if it isn't in perfect balance. But as we tell our three daughters, our goal isn't fairness, our goal is to give each daughter what they need when they need it. They might not want it, but that is parenting, and the same applies to leadership. Forget what your team wants, simply give them what they need. Don't get caught up in the illusion of fairness.

Forget what your team wants, simply give them what they need.

Time shifting

At Xbox, my boss Don Mattrick used to ask this question every time we met: 'Val, did you make more than a week's progress last week?' He would want to know what he could do to speed up how I delivered my goals, what was in the way that he could help move, whether there was anything at risk of not being completed on time, and what else I needed to do to improve the probability of success.

Ten years later, I have never had an executive tell me 'We are moving too fast!' It is always the opposite. The question is how to shift time to your advantage, given your exponential growth goals.

Too often executives treat two-way-door decisions like irreversible one-way-door ones. During my corporate days at Amazon I learned that's how Jeff Bezos categorizes decisions: either they are one-way or two-way, as explained in Chapter 6. You have to assess your Performance Progress Pace (The Triple P) so you and your executive team can have a realistic view of the probability that you will achieve everything you have promised your board and shareholders.

FIGURE 11.2 The Triple P Assessment

	Creative	Technical	Business
Performance Your goals, objectives, financial metrics	●	●	●
Pace Speed of movement to hit agreed timing	●	●	●
Progress Rate of innovation and exploring bold possibilities vs. taking orders	●	●	●

Key
● Significant concerns (red)   Lacking in confidence (yellow)   ● On track and delighted (green)

Use the Triple P Assessment (Figure 11.2) to assess by function how effective each area is and rate them: Red – Significant concerns; Yellow – Lacking in confidence; Green – On track and delighted.

- **Performance** – your goals, objectives, financial metrics.
- **Pace** – the speed at which you are moving so you will hit the agreed-upon time scales.
- **Progress** – you are innovating and developing future possibilities, not just taking orders and doing the minimum possible.

I've worked with companies where the marketing team have an all green PPP score but the technology team's is all red, so the company is not making a month's worth of progress each month. This tool helps you to quickly identify which area is holding you back and rapidly course-correct. To further explore this you need to understand what progress looks like at an exponential pace.

Dog years of progress

Not every year at every company is valued equally. Just as a year in a dog's life is equivalent to seven human years, the same can be said for experience in certain companies.

Unlike many Monday-morning armchair pundits writing about corporate life, I can talk from experience having worked for Amazon on their Fashion Leadership Team during explosive growth. We had acquired Zappos and Shopbop, created MyHabit, and were sowing the early seeds of private label offerings. We were also breaking the mold at Amazon with innovative marketing strategies.

That year was the equivalent of ten years at another company. I secured a seven-figure investment in 48 hours, got to sit the other side of the table from Jeff Bezos, and be a part of watching his brilliance at work, while laying the foundations for what became one of the fastest-growing profitable divisions of Amazon.

Everyone asks me what it was like to work at Amazon and whether all the stories are true. The two biggest challenges that Amazon faces is how they appropriately scale back their strategic appetite to meet the reality of their hiring capacity and managing the risk of having Bezos associated with *The Washington Post*. If I was on the Amazon board, I would tell him to extract himself from that investment, as the political ramifications of having both roles are too risky.

Ask yourself this question: am I at a company where I am learning at the rate of dog years or even Amazon years? If not, go back to Chapter 7 and explore how you can increase the quality and quantity of ideas and see where you can spark more innovation, so you can springboard and accelerate your speed of growth. Finally, in the next chapter, we will explore how to take the thoughts from this book and translate them into rapid action.

CHAPTER 11 RAPID RECAP

1 Reflect on why you need to keep setting resolutions rather than repeating the same ones.

2 Create goals that you will NOT achieve this year to keep your focus.

3 Give your team their goals before the year starts, not a quarter of the way in.

4 Create quarterly progress check-ins for everyone to see progress.

5 Understand how every goal impacts profit, revenue, market share and customers.

6 Know your own satellite navigation system of progress and your ETA.

7 Unfairly allocate how you invest your time and focus your attention.

8 Ask if your team made a week's worth of progress this week.

9 Ensure you deeply understand the financial implications of your budget-planning process.

10 Be transparent with your creative, technical and business peers when creating and monitoring your goals.

CHAPTER TWELVE

Pro tips for fast implementation

'Mind the gap' is the obvious warning on the London Underground as you leave the train and step on the platform, but the gap between today's activities and future opportunity is where many people fall down. This chapter explains how you can take immediate action today and create an early-warning system to ensure your good intentions don't fall through the gap. It covers the common excuses that leaders give for not accelerating innovation, how to overcome them and how to course-correct along the way. Finally, it prepares you for the success you are about to experience as you generate rapid, endless growth.

CHAPTER TOPICS
- Improving your probability of action
- Overcoming fear
- Where to go from here

Improving your probability of action

You may have completed the exercises along the way, or you may need to go back and review the Ideas Instigators at the end of each chapter. Here is the harsh truth about new ideas. There is a Triple S Success approach for implementation success:

- **Say it** If you say out loud what you want to change, you increase the probability that you will actually do it because you have verbalized your intentions.
- **Share it** If you share your intentions and actions, your probability of success further increases because you are building in accountability that someone else can hold you to.
- **Speedily implement it** If you take action in the first 24 hours of learning something new, it will likely stick. If you leave it longer than 24 hours, it will just get added to your long to-do list that should really be labeled to-don't!

I shared these Triple S Success tips at Ingram Micro's Trust X Alliance event where I had just completed an innovation insights interview with Mark Essayian, president of technology firm KME Systems, and he shared how he had already recorded a video about an insight he had from the morning's program and sent it to his team. It was his way of saying it, sharing it and acting with speed.

Here are some further tips to help you implement all that you have learned and achieve rapid growth.

Mind the gap tip 1: Your personal prioritization filter

As a small business owner, Mark Essayian has to ruthlessly prioritize his time. He shared with me how he has the numbers 1, 2, 3 and 4 written on sticky notes on his computer monitor. He uses them to start his action list in the following order:

1 What do I need to do for my clients?
2 What do I need to do for my employees?
3 What do I need to do for my business?
4 What do I need to do for myself?

As Mark explained, 'This allows me to ruthlessly prioritize, because I cannot be working on something for myself if my client is waiting for me.'

Mind the gap tip 2: Replacing old habits with new

We are all creatures of habit. Watch anyone as they enter Starbucks for their morning coffee, or where they sit in a conference room for a regular meeting, or where they park in the car park every day. We repeat common patterns because they are familiar; we simply move into autopilot without even thinking.

Perhaps by now you are considering your habits and have determined which you want to keep and which you are ready to change. I'm working with one executive who has recently taken over his boss's job and now works directly for the CEO. He is breaking not just his own habits but company habits that his predecessor built in the following areas:

• the way strategic choices are made and executed;
• the way acquisitions are evaluated and decided;
• the way his division is energized and inspired by how he interacts with all 3,000 employees.

To break these company habits, he has to change his own habits around how he influences, manages his time and leads his organization. He is completing a reboot of how he works and the altitude he works at.

To successfully adopt new habits you need visual triggers and accountability. Last year I adopted a new habit of cycling my girls to school each morning and then cycling on to CrossFit.

My cycling helmet serves as my morning visual trigger, and my two nine-year-olds are my energetic reminders, who hold me accountable when I'm tempted to sleep in for an extra 15 minutes and take the car!

As you consider all of the new ideas from this book, what habits are you ready to let go of and take on?

Mind the gap tip 3: The Peloton bike pace-setter

I confess that I might be slightly obsessed with my Peloton bike. One of the main reasons for this, beyond the convenience of it sitting in my office, is that it sets the pace for my workout. Sure I'm competitive, but I'm also realistic about their leaderboard, so I compete with myself. I want to beat my personal record for each workout. The tracking and monitoring allow me to do that. Sometimes I can smash one of my records and other times, like this morning, before writing this chapter, I can miss it by 30 per cent. The same applies to your work. You need to know what pace to hit. Sometimes it isn't your own pace. Sometimes you need someone outside your organization comparing you to the best of the best in other leading companies around the world. I often let my executive clients know when they are far exceeding results and performance than I've seen anywhere else, and when they are lagging behind. Who is monitoring your ability and output and helping you adjust?

I was talking to a chief financial officer client of mine last week and as we were recapping her achievements, she quietly said, 'You know, Val, I did most of these in the 45 minutes before our call, as I didn't want to come on here and report I hadn't done them!'

I often hear that the most productive hour of an executive's week is the hour immediately prior to our calls or meetings as they review and prepare. If you don't have anyone helping set the right pace and measuring your progress, how do you know how well you are performing?

Mind the gap tip 4: Words of encouragement when you need it most

'You only sing when you're winning!' is a popular chant sung by British football fans at most matches. It's sung as a cruel taunt to the fans of the opposing team when they are losing and fall silent, no longer cheering on their team. But if you have ever seen LAFC fans, that isn't something you can accuse them of – especially this season's local derby between LAFC and LA Galaxy. As an LAFC season ticket holder, I was part of the 3252, named after the capacity of the North End terrace where supporters sing, chant, dance and cheer their team, whether winning or losing. It's fortunate LAFC fans don't only sing when we are winning, because we were 3–1 down after 16 minutes, but the singing, chanting, drum beating and cheering continued. Considering this team is in their second season, the supporters are incredible. The atmosphere rivals the passion and excitement of English and European stadiums. It reminded me of watching AC Milan versus Inter Milan in the San Siro Stadium many years ago. The crowd can make the game.

Now consider your team at work. How much encouragement do they receive? I don't mean empty 'great job' accolades. No. I mean genuine acts of encouragement and support. Do you give it? Does your boss give it? Does your team need more encouragement where they might not be winning right now?

As for the LAFC derby game, we went on to bring the game to a 3–3 draw and missed far too many chances to actually beat them. But no one could accuse us of only singing when we were winning. Can you say the same for your team?

Mind the gap tip 5: Positive reinforcement

'Yes, that is exactly how you need to be doing that' is a phrase that executives rarely hear. Board advisors, peers, industry gurus and even innovation experts like me are full of advice for executives. But sometimes you simply need to hear some encouragement:

- 'Yes you have got this.'
- 'That is exactly right.'
- 'Yes, spot on.'

With a misplaced desire to be helpful, you can actually over-whelm with advice.

Where do you get your injection of positivity?

Earlier this year I attended the Million Dollar Consulting Hall of Fame event with my mentor Alan Weiss, and it occurred to me while I was talking about my business with 15 of the most successful consultants from around the world that we all need a frequent injection of confidence, reassurance, inspiration, support and praise. Just like executives, consultants cannot do this solo; it is too lonely. Where do you get your injection of positivity?

Mind the gap tip 6: Shifting from knowing to doing

Many executives ask me the same question: 'Val, how can I go from knowing what I need to do to actually doing it?' We know we need to spend more time on our two-year-out zone but we get dragged into issues in the 30-day zone. We know we need to say 'no' more than 'yes', but we agree to more than we should. We know we need to tackle the mismatched employee, but we delay it. We know we need to have the tough conversation but avoid it.

Research shows that if you haven't done something you want to do in 30 days, you need to get help to do it. Here's what you need to know, in order to help you do:

- First, you need to know why you don't.
- Then you need to know what is stopping you.
- Finally, you need to acquire the skills, capability or account-ability to do it.

What's getting in your way?

Mind the gap tip 7: Know what holds back your decisions

I rarely come across an executive who makes decisions too fast. I recently started working with an executive and she said, 'Val, I've achieved more in the last four weeks than the previous four months. You've unlocked decisions I had sat on, freeing up my team to deliver.' We delay for many reasons, but the most common one is confidence:

> *I rarely come across an executive who makes decisions too fast.*

- Are you confident it is the right decision?
- Are you confident that others will agree?
- Are you confident that it won't need changing later?
- Are you confident in your ability to make the right call?

Are your lawyers and HR folks running the business or are you? It's far easier to make a decision work than to keep wringing your hands over what decision to make. The impact of your decisions are far-reaching, but the impact of your indecision is far worse. Don't sacrifice your profits or encourage your people to run out of the door.

What decisions are you holding back on right now that you need to move on?

Mind the gap tip 8: Overcoming barriers

We all have moments in our careers when we have to rise to occasions that feel as though they will be our undoing. Here are some worst-case scenarios that I have seen executives overcome:

- I don't have anywhere near the resources I did in my last company.
- My executive supporters have all left and now I am on my own.
- The acquisition has minimized the scope of my role.
- The person I hired isn't turning out to be as promised.

- The complexity of my new role is enormous compared to what I was told.
- I could feature my current boss in a weekly Dilbert cartoon and still not cover everything they do wrong.

Sound familiar? These are just a few of the common themes I have heard from executives in the last couple of months.

It is easy to feel the weight of disappointment, and when that happens, many executives get stuck in the corporate equivalent of quicksand. Flailing your arms and legs will actually exacerbate your situation and you will sink faster. The same applies in corporate life. Don't run around in angst about your terrible situation; instead, follow these three simple steps:

- **Face your current reality** Talk with someone you trust and outline exactly what is reality and what you are exaggerating in your head.
- **Map out your options** I often ask executives: 'Are you ready to quit?' That frames an option that we all can choose, to simply walk away. If that is not an immediate option, you know you have to work to find a solution.
- **Confront the issue head-on** Talk to your boss, your board or to the appropriate person wherever the issue lies. Explain what you see and how you want to resolve it. Often the solution is far closer and easier than you think.

Remember, flailing your arms won't just cause you to sink deeper in the quicksand, it will pull down your team and everyone else around you.

Overcoming fear

There are few fears we face in our life that truly warrant the feelings that go with them. Yet fear looms large in our ability to mind the gap and embrace rapid growth.

My fear at the top of a double-diamond black ski run is different from my fear of writing on a new topic I never have spoken about before and wondering how people will react. I recently wrote about being a woman executive[1] and I deleted it over and over again until my mentor, Alan Weiss, told me to just submit it to the *Los Angeles Business Journal*, which not only resulted in it being published, but also landed me a new regular weekly column.[2]

Real fear was a day back in 1993 when I was working in Rackhams department store during my corporate days in England; there was an attacker on the shop floor literally cutting the throats of my co-workers. Real fear was when I was put on bed rest for 16 weeks when pregnant with twins and I had an 18-month old running around. Real fear is being diagnosed with a rare auto-immune condition that could have resulted in me losing my eyesight and being in a wheelchair. I don't talk about those fears because they are insignificant compared to the tragedies and difficulties others have faced. But they put into perspective the fears that consume people's decisions to quit a job, try something new, move to a new city or country or simply say what they really think.

When I am advising CEOs, board members, executives and entrepreneurs on growth strategies for their businesses, what is often behind their questions are fears like these. Have you ever experienced any of these fears?

- fear that you will make a mistake;
- fear that you will look needy;
- fear of trying an alternative way rather than your usual approach;
- fear that you will pick the wrong path;
- fear that your outrageous idea may not pan out;
- fear that your hiring bet may fall through.

It isn't the same kind of fear that is life-threatening but it is success-threatening because it causes you to freeze, doubt yourself and perhaps not go as fast as you could.

What do you secretly fear and what is honestly causing it? This was one of the topics I talked about with my incredibly talented sister-in-law, who recently overcame her fear and quit her successful career with a Mercedes Benz group dealership and now has launched her own photography company, Sally Dreams Photography. It occurred to me that there are a number of essentials that executives *need*, but neglect to focus on until it is too late. Here are five of the top 'I wish I had knowns' that I've heard from executives. Keep them in mind so you can get ahead.

Consider how many board members, CEOs or people you know who could hire you.

Don't forget your former colleagues and connections

I had a lovely note from one of my favorite former colleagues and clients. We are now back in touch and he acknowledged his *'benign-neglect-to-awkward-embarrassment cycle of managing my connections with folks who I'm not tightly engaged with on a day-to-day basis.'* He isn't alone. It takes discipline and selfish prioritization to stay connected with those who inspire and energize you but aren't part of your regular cycle of daily activity.

What to do right now Pick three names of those on your regretfully neglected list and call or text them – immediately. Arrange a call or a time to meet up.

Have mentors at the right altitude for your current success

This is easier earlier in your career, when mentors abound everywhere above you. As you rise the ranks to executive, those who can help you are found in a smaller pool and have increasing demands on their time. Look around you now and consider who you call for advice. Do they have the BTDTGR (been-there-done-that-got-results) T-shirt?

What to do right now Consider the future of your business, what is the biggest area that you have never tackled before and ask yourself who has and who could be an advisor to you. If you don't know them, who does? Which one of those people can give you an introduction?

Know people who could hire you

If you haven't already spotted it, yes there is a common theme around evaluating and maintaining connections here. It is the number one theme of complaints from executives on the move. Again, as you move higher, your network requires a different level of seniority.

What to do right now Consider how many board members, CEOs or people you know who could hire you. Is that a dehydrated list? Consider who is one click away who could introduce you.

Don't dive down your internal corporate rabbit warren

I recently invited an executive to keynote at a prominent executive event and he declined because he needed to focus on his newly gained CEO role. While logically I understand his call, there is a danger when you focus too narrowly on internal activities in your first year in a role that requires a dual focus with your external profile.

What to do right now Pick one or two events a year that you decide to invest your time in, either as a speaker or attendee. Want some recommendations? Email or call me and I can tailor specific recommendations just for you.

Be brilliant at sharing your honest brilliance

Before you roll your eyes at the thought of bragging, please hear this: I am constantly amazed at the brilliant – yet secret – achievements of the executives I meet. I recently looked at the CV of a brilliant executive, and her achievements were incredible. But when I googled her, I couldn't find her, and none of the details were on her LinkedIn profile. Sadly, this is a trend rather than a one-off. Reply if you want my fast tips for discovering how amazing you are and how to make sure the virtual you reflects the real you!

CHAPTER 12 RAPID RECAP

1 Say it, share it, implement it within 24 hours for rapid success.

2 Create your own personal prioritization filter and apply it every day.

3 Establish visual triggers to replace old habits with new.

4 Have your eye on a pace-setter that will increase your speed.

5 Find those who encourage as much as critique.

6 Know what holds back your decisions and let it go.

7 Have expert help to overcome your barriers.

8 Internal execution without external focus will stunt your growth.

9 Become brilliant at sharing your honest brilliance.

10 Let people know that you care.

Where to go from here

Winds change fast in corporate life. You can go from being at the top of your game with an abundance of cheerleaders to floating adrift – and alone – just as a result of one or two executive changes or an unexpected acquisition.

Unlike my young daughters, I receive no satisfaction from the *I-told-you-so!* game. If you follow the advice in this book, it can help you prevent regrets from spinning out of your control. Find me online at www.rapidgrowthdoneright.com, I'd love to hear about your rapid growth done right, because, like Mark Essayian, I give a damn about your success.

Endnotes

1 https://www.bizjournals.com/losangeles/news/2017/10/25/what-i-have-learned-from-25-years-of-being-the.html (archived at https://perma.cc/246R-PR9Q)

2 https://www.bizjournals.com/bizjournals/bio/39675/Val+Wright (archived at https://perma.cc/ZY8A-PWQP)

Index